THE ORTHODOX BIBLE STUDY COMPANION
SERIES

THE EPISTLE TO THE HEBREWS

High Priest in Heaven

by Fr. Lawrence R. Farley

Ancient Faith Publishing
Chesterton, Indiana

THE EPISTLE TO THE HEBREWS
Hight Priest in Heaven
© Copyright 2013 by Lawrence Farley

One volume of *The Orthodox Bible Study Companion Series*

All rights reserved. No part of this publication may be reproduced by any means, electronic, mechanical, photocopying, recording, scanning, or otherwise, without the prior written permission of the publisher.

Published by   Ancient Faith Publishing
                A Division of Ancient Faith Ministries
                P.O. Box 748
                Chesterton, IN 46304

ISBN: 978-1-936270-74-3

Printed in the United States of America

Dedicated to the memory of
"Papa" John Scratch,
with admiration, gratitude, and love

Table of Contents and Outline

Introduction to the Series 7
   A Word about Scholarship and Translation ✥ 7
   Key to the Format of This Work ✥ 9

Introduction: The Puzzle of the Episle 11

I. Prologue (1:1–4) 19

II. Christ Superior to the Angels (1:5—2:18) 25
   1. The Son Superior to the Angels (1:5–14) ✥ 25
   2. Christ's Word Greater than the Law Given through Angels (2:1–4) ✥ 34
   3. Christ Made Lower than the Angels to Suffer Death as High-Priest (2:5–18) ✥ 37

III. Christ Our High-Priest (3:1—10:18) 45
   1. Christ Greater than Moses (3:1–6) ✥ 45
   2. Beware Lest You Fall Away from Christ's Sabbath Rest (3:7—4:13) ✥ 48
   3. Christ Our High-Priest (4:14—5:10) ✥ 57
   4. Press On to Maturity (5:11—6:20) ✥ 66
   5. Christ a High-Priest like Melchizedek (7:1–28) ✥ 82
   6. Christ's Priesthood Greater than Aaron's (8:1—10:18) ✥ 93

IV. Hold Fast to Christ (10:19—12:29) 123
   1. Do Not Draw Back from Christian Worship (10:19–39) ✥ 123
   2. Hold Fast to Faith as the Fathers Did (11:1—12:2) ✥ 133
   3. Accept Suffering as God's Sons (12:3–29) ✥ 150

V. Conclusion (13:1–25) 163
    1. Final Admonitions (13:1–19) ⚜ 163
    2. Concluding Blessing (13:20–21) ⚜ 172
    3. Final Greetings (13:22–25) ⚜ 173

Excurses (short expositions on various topics):
- On the Use of the Septuagint 32
- On the Interpretation of Psalm 2:7 64
- On the Tabernacle and Temple as Antitypes......................... 95
- On the Abolition of the Old Covenant.............................. 100
- On the Significance of the Temple Furnishings................... 104
- On the Sacrifice of Christ and on the Eucharist 120
- On the Wrath of God 128

About the Author 175
Also in the Series 176
Other Books by the Author 177

❦ Introduction to the Series ❧

A Word about Scholarship and Translation
This commentary was written for your grandmother. And for your plumber, your banker, your next-door neighbor, and the girl who serves you French fries at the nearby McDonald's. That is, it was written for the average layman, for the nonprofessional who feels a bit intimidated by the presence of copious footnotes, long bibliographies, and all those other things which so enrich the lives of academics. It is written for the pious Orthodox layman who is mystified by such things as Source Criticism, but who nonetheless wants to know what the Scriptures mean.

Therefore, it is unlike many other commentaries, which are written as contributions to the ongoing endeavor of scholarship and as parts of a continuous dialogue among scholars. That endeavor and dialogue is indeed worthwhile, but the present commentary forms no part of it. For it assumes, without argument, a certain point of view, and asserts it without defense, believing it to be consistent with the presuppositions of the Fathers and therefore consistent with Orthodox Tradition. It has but one aim: to be the sort of book a busy parish priest might put in the hands of an interested parishioner who says to him over coffee hour after Liturgy, "Father, I'm not sure I really get what St. Paul is saying in the Epistles. What does it all mean?" This commentary tries to tell the perplexed parishioner what the writers of the New Testament mean.

Regarding the translation used herein, an Italian proverb says, "All translators are traitors." (The proverb proves its own point, for it sounds better in Italian!) The point of the proverb, of course, is that no translation, however careful, can bring out all the nuances and meanings of the original, since no language can be the mathematical equivalent of another. The English translator is faced, it would seem, with a choice: either he can make the translation something of a

7

rough paraphrase of the original and render it into flowing sonorous English; or he can attempt to make a fairly literal, word-for-word translation from the original with the resultant English being stilted, wooden, and clumsy.

These two basic and different approaches to translation correspond to two basic and different activities in the Church. The Church needs a translation of the Scriptures for use in worship. This should be in good, grammatical, and flowing English, as elegant as possible and suited to its function in the majestic worship of the Liturgy. The Church also needs a translation of the Scriptures for private study and for group Bible study. Here the elegance of its English is of lesser concern. What is of greater concern here is the bringing out of all the nuances found in the original. Thus this approach will tend to sacrifice elegance for literality and, wherever possible, seek a word-for-word correspondence with the Greek. Also, because the student will want to see how the biblical authors use a particular word (especially St. Paul, who has many works included in the canon), a consistency of translation will be sought and the same Greek word will be translated, wherever possible, by the same English word or by its cognate.

The present work does not pretend to be anything other than a translation for private Bible study. It seeks to achieve, as much as possible, a literal, word-for-word correspondence with the Greek. The aim has been to present a translation from which one could jump back into the Greek original with the aid of an interlinear New Testament. Where a single Greek word has been used in the original, I have tried to find (or invent!) a single English word.

The result, of course, is a translation so literally rendered from the Greek that it represents an English spoken nowhere on the planet! That is, it represents a kind of "study Bible English" and not an actual vernacular. It was never intended for use outside the present commentaries, much less in the worship of the Church. The task of producing a flowing, elegant translation that nonetheless preserves the integrity and nuances of the original I cheerfully leave to hands more competent than mine.

Key to the Format of This Work:
- The translated text is first presented in boldface type. Italics within these biblical text sections represent words required by English syntax that are not actually present in the Greek. Each translated text section is set within a shaded grey box.

> ❧ ❧ ❧ ❧ ❧
> 8   But of the Son *he says*: "Your throne, O God, is to ages of ages, and the righteous staff *is* the staff of Your Kingdom.

- In the commentary sections, citations from the portion of text being commented upon are given in boldface type.

  These descriptions of the Son contrast sharply with the Scripture's portrayal of the angels. For **of the angels He says, "Who makes His angels winds and His offerers a flame of fire."** This passage from the Greek of Psalm 104:4 reflects how the author uses his Old Testament sources.

- In the commentary sections, citations from other locations in Scripture are given in quotation marks with a reference; any reference not including a book name refers to the book under discussion.

  If anyone "sinned with a high hand" (Num. 15:30), defiantly repudiating the divine covenant, that person was to be "cut from the people" and killed.

- In the commentary sections, italics are used in the ordinary way—for emphasis, foreign words, etc.

  The word for *angels* is a bit elastic in both the Hebrew and the Greek, as is the word for *winds*.

❧ Introduction ❧

THE PUZZLE OF THE EPISTLE

To speak of an "epistle to the Hebrews" is in itself to go out on a limb somewhat, because the work commonly known by that title does not have the form of an epistle, and it nowhere actually claims to be written to the Hebrews. When we refer to "the Epistle to the Hebrews," we are already relying upon the Tradition of the Church.

Epistles in antiquity all began with a statement of who the author was and who the intended recipients were, and conveyed some sort of greeting. An epistle might begin (for example), "Paul, an apostle of Jesus Christ and Timothy our brother, to the saints and faithful brothers in Colossae: grace to you" (Col. 1:1–2). Or it might begin, "The apostles and the brothers who are elders, to the brothers in Antioch, greetings" (Acts 15:23).

In the present work, there is no epistolary opening like this at all. We do not know for sure who wrote it or from where, to whom this person wrote it, or where they lived, or why it was written, or when. As Origen once said, the authorship of the epistle "is known to God alone" (quoted by Eusebius in his *History of the Church*, 6, 25).

That has not stopped anyone, however (including Origen), from hazarding an opinion.

Clement of Alexandria (who died about 215) felt that Paul was indeed the writer, but that he omitted giving his name in the usual epistolary opening because "he was far too sensible to put off his readers at the start by naming himself," since "the Hebrews were already prejudiced against him and suspicious of him." Clement was head of a great catechetical school at Alexandria, and he says that his view was shared by his predecessor there, the "blessed Elder" Pantaenus (cited by Eusebius, *History of the Church*, 6.14).

Origen himself (who died about 254) guessed that an early disciple of Paul wrote the book, giving a disciple's interpretation to what his master Paul had earlier taught (quoted by Eusebius in his *History*, 6.25). After Origen, the Christian East in general accepted the epistle as canonical and as Pauline in authorship.

Another early opinion was that St. Barnabas wrote it. Tertullian, who died about 240, said (in his work *On Modesty*, ch. 20) that "there is extant an epistle to the Hebrews under the name of Barnabas." Though Tertullian states this as an established fact, there is no trace of the epistle actually bearing the name of Barnabas, and it seems that this is simply Tertullian's guess.

The Roman Church at the time of Eusebius (that is, in the early fourth century) also denied that this epistle was Pauline, and this influenced others (compare Eusebius, *History*, 3.3). The epistle was omitted from the early African Canon, and St. Cyprian of Carthage (d. 258) never mentions it. It was not until the work of St. Jerome and St. Augustine in the early fifth century that the West in general came to accept the epistle.

What can we say about the work with reasonable certainty? I would suggest the following:

1. It seems clear that it was not written by Paul. The style and vocabulary are quite different from all his other epistles, and Paul himself says he personally signed all his works as a sign of authenticity (2 Thess. 3:17). With all due respect to Clement of Alexandria, it is difficult to think that one of Paul's temperament would have shrunk from naming himself at the beginning of his work for any reason whatsoever.
2. It also seems clear that it was written within the second generation from Christ and His apostles, at a time somewhat later than Paul's. In 2:3 the author seems to look back to the apostles, referring to them as "those who heard" what the Lord had spoken and who "confirmed it to us." This would be an odd way for an apostle of the first generation to speak, but reads quite

naturally from someone in the second generation. Also, in 13:7, the author of the work bids his readers to consider their leaders' end of life (Gr. *ekbasis*, compare its use in Wisdom 2:17), and this also suggests that some time had elapsed during which those leaders had died. Further, by the time this epistle was written, Timothy had been imprisoned and then released (13:23); these events are hard to fit into the chronology of the first generation. They suggest a time after the martyrdom of Paul, which took place in the mid-sixties. For all these reasons, it seems clear that this epistle was written by someone belonging to the second generation of Christians.

3. It seems certain that the work was written before the Temple was destroyed in AD 70. The author argues that the Old Covenant with its Temple rites has become old and is ready to disappear (8:13). If the Temple had in fact disappeared, the writer would certainly have mentioned this as the clinching part of his argument. The fact that he did *not* mention it shows that at the time of writing, the Temple was still standing.

4. Finally, it seems beyond dispute that the recipients were Jews (or Hebrews), for all the argument deals with difficulties only a Jew would have. The recipients then were Christian Jews (that is, Jews who were baptized members of the Church).

This much, then, seems certain. Building upon this, I would also suggest the following as a possible scenario.

1. The Author: The epistle was written by an otherwise unknown and anonymous Christian teacher of the second generation. This lack of fame alone accounts for the subsequent uncertainty and debate over authorship, for if it had been written by a famous apostle (such as Paul, Barnabas, Silas, or Luke), this notable fact would surely have survived along with the epistle itself. The widespread uncertainty regarding authorship seems to me to witness unmistakably that it was *not* written by such a famous person. When we moderns guess at authorship, of course we make our selection from the list of famous apostolic persons whose works have survived and whom we know.

But there is nothing to say that the epistle could not have been written by someone who otherwise remained completely unknown.

Further, our author was in Italy at the time of writing (compare 13:24, where the author sends greetings "from those of Italy"), probably in Rome itself, since he was aware of the recent release of Timothy from prison (13:23). Though word of this release would have spread to regions other than Rome, those in Rome would be the first to know, and it could well be that our author was reporting the latest news.

2. The Recipients: I would also suggest that the Hebrew Christians intended as recipients were those from the churches of Palestine. It was in Palestine that the Christian Jews were most persecuted by their unbelieving Jewish countrymen (compare 1 Thess. 2:14), and the epistle clearly supposes a high level of persecution (10:32–34).

Also, the author of the epistle does not rebuke his audience for abandoning their Gentile Christian brothers. If the Christian Jews addressed in the epistle were those of the Diaspora outside of Palestine, the Jewish Christians would have been mixed in with Gentile Christians in those churches, and staying away from the Christian Eucharist would have meant separating from the Gentile Christians who remained there. We know that the author does rebuke his readers for their temptation to stay away from the Eucharist (10:25), but there is no suggestion that by so doing they are abandoning their brothers. The churches addressed seem to have been composed entirely of Hebrew Christians, and this was true only in Palestine.

Further, it seems likely that a specific community was intended, perhaps the members of a house church, and that the epistle was not intended for general circulation. There are many references to the readers' past experience, and these are specific and personal. They presuppose that our author knew them intimately (see 5:11–14; 6:9–12; 10:32–35; 12:4; 13:19, 23). This reads more naturally of a specific group than of a generalized audience.

3. The Occasion: I suggest that our author was a Jewish Christian teacher in Rome who had connections with these Jewish Christians in Palestine. He had heard that his friends there were experiencing some difficulty and were tempted to withdraw from the Faith.

They had indeed experienced persecution, had been plundered of their goods, and some had been imprisoned (10:34), though none had yet been martyred (12:4). They were being pressured by their fellow Jews who did not believe in Christ to fall away from their Christian allegiance back into simple Judaism (12:3). It is even possible they were being threatened with expulsion from the Temple worship (13:10–15). These Christian Jews perhaps thought if they did renounce Christ, their participation in the Temple sacrifices would still avail them (10:26–31).

Faced with all this pressure, they had begun to consider forsaking the Christian eucharistic assembly on the first day of the week, as others had done (10:25). They were also worried by the financial difficulty their Christian faith had brought them (13:5–6). Moreover, some were beginning to slide into sexual immorality (12:15–17; 13:4). They were also quarreling with their fellow Christians (12:14), especially with their Christian leaders (13:17, 24).

The author of this epistle therefore wrote to his friends in Palestine, urging them not to fall away from their Christian allegiance. As Christian Jews, they went on the Sabbath to synagogue with all their other Jewish compatriots (both Christian and non-Christian), and then on the first day of the week gathered with their fellow Christian Jews for the Eucharist. With the pressure these Christian Jews were getting from their non-Christian Jewish brothers, they were contemplating ceasing to attend the Sunday Eucharist. It seems as if they were tempted not so much to openly and decisively deny that Jesus was the Messiah as to do nothing about it.

Today we tend to think of Judaism and Christianity as two separate religions, between which one must choose. But the Jews to whom this epistle was written did not think of Christianity as separate from their Judaism. Rather, they considered that their ancestral Jewish faith was fulfilled in their following of Jesus as the Messiah. They were still Jews and believed themselves acceptable to God because they were Jews. They still practiced all the Jewish rites of circumcision and food laws, of Torah study and Temple worship.

As followers of the Way (Acts 24:14), their Christian allegiance was but a part of their Jewishness. As they considered stepping back from outward allegiance to Jesus as Messiah, to their minds they were not abandoning Christianity for Judaism so much as they were simply deemphasizing one (controversial) part of their total faith. They did not regard this as apostasy from the God of Israel. After all, they were still good Jews.

In response to this danger, the author of the epistle undertakes to show the importance of Jesus for their salvation and thereby to show that falling away from Jesus does indeed involve falling away from all that the God of Israel had provided for their salvation. If they "deemphasized" the Christian part of their faith by refraining from assembling for the Eucharist (10:25), this overthrew everything. Apostasy from their Christian confession meant apostasy from God, and no amount of Temple sacrifice could save them (10:26–31).

The author therefore takes pains to reveal who Jesus is: higher than the angels, more important than Moses, with a ministry more exalted and effective than the high priest offering sacrifice in the Jerusalem Temple. If holding to their faith in Jesus meant they were banished from synagogue and Temple, they must hold to their faith nonetheless, for in Jesus they had a salvation and a high priest superior to the earthly high priest in Jerusalem.

Along with holding to their faith in Jesus (expressed by their assembling for the Eucharist), they must also live out that faith, resisting temptations to sexual immorality and living in peace with their leaders, trusting in God to provide for them. The author of the epistle aims at nothing less than the complete dedication of his hearers to Christ as the center of their lives and their only hope.

4. The Place and Date of Writing: This epistle was written, I suggest, from Rome, Italy, about the year 67. This would place the time of writing after the death of Paul and the subsequent imprisonment and release of Timothy, but before the destruction of the Temple in AD 70. If this supposition about the date is correct, it would explain the persecution the Christian Jews were experiencing at the hands of their non-Christian Jewish compatriots; for during these years, the struggle of the Jews of Palestine with Rome was increasingly intense, and Christian Jews would have been under great pressure to show their Jewish patriotism. Their faith in Jesus as the Messiah set them apart from the rest of their compatriots, and these divisions would have been resented by those who felt that all Jews must now stand together in a united front against Rome.

5. The Original Language and the Omission of the Epistolary Opening: It would seem the epistle was originally composed in Greek (and not translated into Greek from an Aramaic original). Not only is the Greek very polished, but the author makes use of the Greek Septuagint version when he quotes the Old Testament Scriptures, and this would less likely be the case if he were writing in Aramaic.

I suggest that the epistle originally did contain an epistolary opening greeting, but that this was omitted by the first copyist when it was copied and sent out for wider circulation. If the author and his addressees were otherwise unknown Christians, their names in the opening greeting would be meaningless to the wider audience, and so the greeting was simply dropped.

The Epistle to the Hebrews continues to attract ingenious guesswork from scholars today. We should not let its puzzles, however, detract our attention from the excellences of the work. Whoever wrote it and whoever were its intended recipients, the work remains in the Church as a precious legacy from the first Christians, transmitting the authentic teaching of the apostles to the Church of later ages. It is to the author of this work that the Church owes much of its insight into the high-priesthood of Jesus Christ—the One who remains in the heavens on our behalf, the same yesterday, today, and forever.

I

PROLOGUE
(1:1–4)

The Christian readers of the epistle all acknowledged that Jesus was the Messiah, but they still needed to know what this meant. Some may have thought Messiah was simply a prophet—greater than all the other prophets, to be sure, but basically still just a man and no more. Others may have thought the Messiah was a kind of incarnate angel, since the angels were the highest category of created being they knew of. This idea was made more attractive by the title given the Messiah in the Greek version of Isaiah 9:6, the "Angel of Great Counsel."

The author of this work therefore first begins to explain the greatness of Jesus and that He is not simply an incarnate angel, but is greatly superior to the angels. His greatness is, in fact, the greatness of God Himself. The readers of the epistle were tempted to think they could withdraw from their allegiance to Jesus and this would still leave their Jewish faith more or less unimpaired. The author shows this is not so: Jesus is not simply one in a series of prophets. He is the fullness and culmination of all God has accomplished from the beginning, and the sacred history of Judaism makes no sense without Him.

Thus (the author's main point and motivation in comparing Christ to angels in the following section), Christ's greatness, supremacy, and superiority over anything in Judaism make withdrawal from Him unthinkable. How could the Hebrew Christians even consider abandoning their loyalty to Jesus when He is so exalted?

> ❧ ❧ ❧ ❧ ❧
>
> **1** 1 In many portions and in many ways, God long ago, after He spoke to the fathers in the prophets,
> 2 at the end of these days, spoke to us in *the* Son, whom He appointed heir of all things, through whom also He made the ages.
> 3 He is the radiance of His glory and the representation of His being, and He carries all things by the word of His power. When He had made cleansing of sins, He sat down at the right hand of the Greatness on high,
> 4 having become so much better than the angels, as He has inherited a more outstanding Name than they.

The author begins by placing Jesus in the framework of all God's other self-revelations. **In many portions and in many ways** [the Greek is alliterative: *polumeros kai polutropos*] **God long ago spoke to the fathers in the prophets**. That is, God revealed Himself **in many portions**, sometimes revealing much of His purposes, at other times revealing little. He revealed Himself **in many ways**, using oracles, poetry, parables, visions, proverbs, discourse. This He did through **the prophets** (that is, through all the authors of the Old Testament Scriptures, including Moses, David, Solomon, Isaiah, and the other prophets).

These self-revelations were accurate as far as they went, but they were partial. Now, **at the end of these days**, God **spoke to us in *the* Son**, making a full and complete self-revelation. By saying that God revealed Himself thus **at the end of these days**, our author does not simply mean that He revealed Himself lately or recently. The phrase not only means "in our own time," but also has an eschatological flavor. Christ was revealed in the fullness of time, at the ends of the ages (see 1 Cor. 10:11), as the consummation of human history. All

I. Prologue — Hebrews 1:1–4

previous times and events led up to this culmination, and Christ appears as the fulfillment and key of all that has preceded Him or will follow.

In placing God's self-revelation in His Son at the end of a list of His previous self-disclosures, the author of our epistle stresses the difference between this last self-disclosure and the previous ones. God's Incarnation in Christ is not simply the next in an ongoing series of epiphanies, nor is it just the last one. Christ is not only (as Muslims claim for Mohammed) "the Seal of the Prophets." Rather, the Incarnation forms the climax of God's self-disclosure and revelation throughout history, because in Christ, the Father has fully (and therefore finally) revealed Himself, whereas in all the previous revelations God revealed only something of Himself and His will.

In the visions and communications to the Patriarchs, God revealed His will for all the nations (see Gen. 12:1–3). In His appearance in the thundering fire of Mount Sinai, the invisible God revealed His will to Israel through Moses, giving them the Law. Through the prophets, He revealed His character and His demand for holiness from His people. God spoke by His servants in many and varied literary forms, giving psalms to David, wise proverbs and aphorisms to Solomon (along with love poetry). He gave visions of His glory to Isaiah and Ezekiel, visions of His angelic protection to Zechariah, visions of His judgment among the nations to Daniel. Through the prophets, He spoke in poetic power of the coming Kingdom and its King, the Messiah of the House of David.

All of these visions and Scriptures revealed God's *will*. But this last revelation is different: it reveals and manifests *the living God Himself*, for Christ is the true Son of the Father, the embodiment of all that the invisible Father is in Himself. Thus, God's revelation through His Son brings to an end all possibility of subsequent revelation, because now nothing remains to be revealed. There can be no "latter day" revelation, no "Latter Day Saints," because in Christ all the fullness of God has been revealed. God held nothing back. All that can be known about Him has been made known in Jesus of Nazareth. This final revelation sums up and surpasses all previous revelations and brings the time of revelation to an end.

The author describes this messianic Son in a series of images. We may find it easy today to miss the original shocking significance of these descriptions, accustomed as we are to speaking of Jesus as the Second Person of the Trinity. Our long and easy familiarity with the Nicene Orthodoxy of the Creed can desensitize us so that we miss how scandalous these assertions seemed in the first century. For Christians then (and people generally) began with an understanding not of Jesus' divinity, but of His humanity, and to many it seemed shocking to say that a thirty-year-old carpenter from an obscure town in Palestine who was executed as a criminal is now running the universe. But that is what the Christians asserted. The following descriptions of Jesus would not have been taken for granted by people in the first century. The Christians knew that Jesus of Nazareth was the appointed Messiah and that He exercised divine authority. But His full significance had not entirely sunk in.

Our author first describes Jesus as the one **whom** God **appointed heir of all things**. That is, the carpenter from Nazareth is the One appointed by the Father to inherit the entire age to come. Jesus will not simply enter the age to come; He will rule over it as Lord and Owner of the renewed universe. The Messiah does not merely sit as King over Jewish Palestine, with connections to the Gentile nations. As Messiah He was to "receive the ends of the earth" as His "possession" (Ps. 2:8). Christ Jesus sits as King over the whole cosmos, and nothing remains beyond His saving sway.

Further, this Son is the One **through whom** God **also made the ages**. The Father made the world through His wisdom and His word (Wisdom 9:1–2). Jesus, prior to His Incarnation through the Virgin Theotokos in Bethlehem, lived with the Father as that eternal Word and Wisdom through which the Father made all things, fashioning and planning all that would ever come to be. The author of our epistle, in describing the pre-incarnate Christ as the divine Agent of the Father in creation, attributes deity to the Son as well.

In addition, Christ is **the radiance of** God's **glory**. The word rendered *radiance* (Gr. *apaugasma*) can mean both the passive reflection and also the active effulgence. Both meanings are found here, since the Son is the reflection and expression of the Father.

I. Prologue — Hebrews 1:1–4

In speaking of the relationship between Christ and the Father, the Fathers often use the image of the radiance of the sun: the inner core of the sun's fiery heart expresses itself in the flashing forth of its rays, and one can see the sun only in this effulgence burning in the sky, since its inner core remains inaccessible to human eyes. In the same way, the Son is the expression of the Father's transcendent glory. The Father in Himself remains inaccessible and invisible to His creation, and He is only seen as He manifests Himself through His Son. This is what Christ meant when He said to His disciples, "He who has seen Me has seen the Father" (John 14:9).

Further, Jesus is **the representation of** the Father's **being**. The word translated *representation* is the Greek *character*, the word used for the stamp on seals, cognate with the verb *charasso*, "to engrave." Just as a stamp or seal produces the exact representation of the image on the wax, so the Son is the exact representation and image of the Father's **being**, His nature (Gr. *upostasis*). All that God the Father is the Son is also. The Son bears within Him the full deity of the Father and all His power and authority.

Also, the Son **carries** and upholds **all things** in the universe by the simple **word of His power**. He sustains the whole cosmos by His word of command. Since He is one with the Father and is the One through whom the Father made all things (compare 1 Cor. 8:6), all things continue in existence only because He orders it. The universe is not self-sustaining. It is sustained only by God's power. God works through what scientists describe as "the laws of nature" to maintain the fabric of the cosmos He created. As G. K. Chesterton once wrote, the sun only rises each morning because each morning God bids it rise. Our author asserts that it is the eternal Son who bids it rise; it is the eternal Son in whom all things hold together (compare Col. 1:17).

And the Son is not simply one with the Father in His greatness as Creator. He also rules as the triumphant Savior and Redeemer. After **He had made cleansing of sins** by His death on the Cross and swept sin from the universe, **He sat down at the right hand of the Greatness** (that is, the Father; the Jews often used such circumlocutions for God) and remains there, exalted **on high**. To say

23

that Jesus **sat down** does not, of course, refer to His physical posture but is a theological assertion of His sovereignty. Jesus now rules as King, sharing the throne and authority of His Father. The Jews of the first century expected Messiah to rule on a throne, but these expectations centered around an earthly throne, ruling an earthly kingdom, a Jewish version of the *Pax Romana*. Christians asserted that Christ possessed an authority far more exalted and that He sat down in heaven at the right hand of God. Christ, though true man and Son of David, rules over the entire universe. Christians confess the truth, shocking to conventional Jewish piety (and to Muslim piety today), that a Man sits enthroned with God, sharing His rule of the world.

As the readers of the epistle could see, Jesus is far more exalted than any angelic being. He has **become so much better than the angels as He has inherited a more outstanding Name** or rank **than they**. In speaking of **inheriting** a **Name**, the author means that Jesus inherits the Father's glory and rank and authority. A son will inherit all the wealth and status of the father, and in the same way Jesus the Son inherits all the power and glory of God the Father when He ascends to His right hand as the triumphant Messiah. Jesus humbled Himself to death on the Cross, but the Father raised Him up and glorified Him to His throne in heaven, in this way causing Jesus to **inherit** His **Name** and glory. This glorification is the measure of the Son's superiority to the angels.

❦ II ❧

CHRIST SUPERIOR TO THE ANGELS
(1:5—2:18)

§II.1. The Son Superior to the Angels (1:5–14)

After asserting the immeasurable superiority of the Son over the angels, the author then proceeds to back up his statement with Scripture in typical Jewish fashion. Once again we must stress that the truth that Christ is superior to the angels seems obvious to us today. Our Orthodox prayer books contain prayers to God and also prayers asking for the angels to intercede for us, and these prayers to the angels show how clearly subordinate the angels are to the Holy Trinity.

But Judaism of the first century did not have the advantage of our Nicene Orthodoxy. The full divinity and consubstantiality of the Son with the Father had not yet been articulated. When the Jewish Christianity of the first century strove to articulate the greatness of the Son, the highest category they possessed was that of the angels. (As said above, the description of Messiah in the Greek version of Isaiah 9:6 referred to Him as "Angel of Great Counsel.") Thus it was but natural that primitive Jewish Christology should refer to Christ as an angel.

In the poetry of Isaiah this was acceptable, but the first-century Church, caught in the crossfire of rapidly evolving Gnosticism, needed to define Christ more precisely, and such poetic descriptions were no longer sufficient. People might misunderstand this term and conclude that Christ was no more than a superior kind of angel—exalted indeed, but created like the rest of the angels. The author of our epistle confronts this tendency and possibility head on, asserting not only the full divinity of Christ, but also His essential difference from the angelic orders.

To do this, he collects a series of Scripture statements about the Messiah and about the angels, presenting them in the form of contrasting pairs so that his readers may observe the contrast for themselves. His point is this: Whenever the Scripture speaks of the Messiah, it always uses the language of sovereignty and eternity, stressing His nearness to the Father. Whenever the Scripture speaks of the angels, however, it uses the language of humble worship and servanthood. Obviously, then, the Messiah cannot be a kind of angel.

> ༄༅ ༄༅ ༄༅ ༄༅ ༄༅
>
> 5 For to which of the angels did He ever say, "You *Yourself* are My Son; today I *Myself* have begotten You"? and again, "I *Myself* will be a Father to him and he *himself* will be a son to Me"?
> 6 And again when He brings the firstborn into the world, He says, "And let all *the* angels of God worship Him."

The author begins by citing a classic text from Psalm 2:7, in which God addresses the Davidic Messiah with the words, **"You *Yourself* are My Son; today I *Myself* have begotten You."** This is coupled with the promise of God to David in 2 Samuel 7:14, **"I *Myself* will be a Father to him and he *himself* will be a son to Me."** (The Greek pronouns are emphatic in these citations.) Both passages were considered to have messianic significance.

God had made spectacular promises to David. He promised him that his dynasty would last forever and that his throne would never be overthrown (2 Sam. 13). He promised him that the foreign enemy would never outwit him and that all his foes would be crushed, that he would reign from the Mediterranean Sea to the Euphrates, and that the Davidic King would be the highest of the kings of the earth (Ps. 89:22, 23, 25, 27). This arrangement would last forever, as eternal as the sun and the moon in the heavens (Ps. 89:36–37).

King David himself did not experience such glory, nor did any of his immediate descendants. Indeed, his earthly sovereignty came to a crashing catastrophic end in the Babylonian Captivity in 586 BC. Since God's word cannot prove false, this glory must be fulfilled in David's descendant, the Messiah. The Messiah would experience that glory. He would know the nearness of a **son** to God, who would protect him as a **Father** would his own offspring (see Ps. 89:26) and fulfill all the promises made to David. The author of the epistle asks rhetorically, **to which of the angels did** God **ever say** something like this? None of the angels was ever portrayed as having such a singularly exclusive relationship to God.

Indeed, the author goes on to say that on the occasion **when** God **brings the firstborn into the world**, the Scripture says, "**Let all *the* angels of God worship Him**" (Deut. 32:43; Ps. 97:7 LXX). **The firstborn** refers to the relationship of the Messiah to the other kings of the earth, for in Psalm 89:27, the Davidic Messiah is described as God's "firstborn, the highest of the kings of the earth," and the Greek word for *world* here is *oikoumene*, used in Luke 2:1 to describe the Roman Empire. Thus, the author is comparing the status of the Messiah to those of all the other kings of earth's empires and saying that Messiah is superior to them all. Indeed, He is so exalted that even *the* **angels of God worship Him**. The Messiah cannot be an angel, for all the angels worship Him, giving to Him the kind of obeisance usually offered only to God.

> ৯৭ ৯৭ ৯৭ ৯৭ ৯৭
> 7 And of the angels He says, "Who makes His angels winds and His offerers a flame of fire."

These descriptions of the Son contrast sharply with the Scripture's portrayal of the angels. For **of the angels He says, "Who makes His angels winds and His offerers a flame of fire."** This passage from the Greek of Psalm 104:4 reflects how the author uses his Old Testament sources. The word for *angels* is a bit elastic in both the Hebrew and the Greek, as is the word for *winds*. The word for *angel* (Heb. *malak*; Gr. *aggelos*) in both languages can mean both "messenger" in general and also "angel." The word for *wind* (Heb. *ruach*; Gr. *pneuma*) can mean both "wind" and "spirit" or "breath." In the original context of Psalm 104:4, the psalmist is talking about Yahweh's sovereignty over the elements and saying that all things serve His purposes—He makes the very winds (*ruach*) His messengers (*malak*), the very flaming fire and lightning His servants.

This notion of the elemental world underwent some development in the centuries that followed, as a deeper understanding of the spiritual component of creation continued to evolve. Many thought the angels—those invisible created ranks who served God in heaven—undergirded the forces of the created world as well, carrying out God's will in creation. Thus the intertestamental *Book of Enoch* (chapter 60) speaks of "the spirit of the sea," "the spirit of the hoarfrost," "the spirit of the hail," "the spirit of the snow." All the powers of nature were perceived as having an angelic guardian who saw to their functions.

This notion appears to be at the back of the author's understanding of Psalm 104:4. Following the Greek Septuagint version, he reads *aggelos* as "angel," not simply as "messenger," and he reads *pneuma* as "wind." According to this reading, the psalmist presents the **angels**, God's **offerers** and priestly servants (Gr. *leitourgos*, the word used to describe the priests of the Old Testament) as becoming **winds** and **a flame of fire** (i.e. lightning) as they carry out God's will. This is consistent with other intertestamental views of the angels. In 2 Esdras 8:22, it says that "at God's command, [the angels] are changed to wind and fire." That is, when God so orders, the angels take the form of wind and lightning as they carry out their functions as guardians of the created order.

What is the significance of this Scripture? The author of the epistle cites it because it underscores the comparatively transient nature of angels. Like winds and lightning, which come and then are gone, so are the angels in their work in this world. They perform the work of **offerers**, of servants, carrying out the will of God for the elements. Theirs is not a ruling role as is that of the Son, who shares the authority of His Father on the earth. Theirs is rather a subordinate role as they humbly watch over the passing powers of creation.

> ࿐ ࿐ ࿐ ࿐ ࿐
>
> 8 But of the Son *he says*: "Your throne, O God, is to ages of ages, and the righteous staff *is* the staff of Your Kingdom.
> 9 "You loved righteousness and hated lawlessness; because of this God, your God, anointed you with the oil of exultation above your partners."
> 10 And "You, O Lord, in the beginning founded the earth, and the heavens are the works of Your hands.
> 11 "They will perish, but You Yourself remain on, and they all will *grow* old as a garment,
> 12 "and as a mantle You will roll them up, as a garment they also will be changed. But You *Yourself* are the same and Your years will not fail."

Our author again contrasts this subordinate role for the angels with that of the Son. For in Psalm 45:6–7 (LXX) it is written, **"Your throne, O God, is to ages of ages, and the righteous staff *is* the staff of Your Kingdom. You loved righteousness and hated lawlessness; because of this God, your God, anointed you with the oil of exultation above your partners."** In its original context, these verses referred to the Davidic king and were written as a praise psalm celebrating the royal marriage. The psalmist praises the king with the usual hyperbolic language of the oriental court and addresses him as if he were divine. The king is addressed as **God** by the psalmist because the power of God had established his **throne** and his dynasty so that it would last **to ages of ages**. Moreover, the king's sovereignty was assured by God, since the king was righteous in his rule (wielding a **righteous staff** or scepter) as he continued to **love righteousness and hate lawlessness**. Since the Davidic king pleased God by his just rule, God in turn **anointed** him **with the oil of exultation**, making him king and raising him **above** his former **partners**, the other kings of the earth.

As said above, the historical House of David never did attain to such political heights, and the final fulfillment of these hopes remained to be found in the Messiah. The author of the epistle quotes this psalm here because it expresses the eternity and sovereignty of the Messiah as contrasted to the subordinate status of the angels. What was spoken of David's house in the language of poetic hyperbole was fulfilled literally in Jesus. In Him poetry, myth, and aspiration become fact and history. The king whose marriage was celebrated in this psalm was God only in a poetic sense, but Jesus was true **God** in actual fact. Jesus' **throne** is indeed **to ages of ages** and He is in fact exalted **above** His **partners**, all other authority and powers—even that of the angels.

This eternity of the Messiah is expressed in another Scripture cited by the author of the epistle, Psalm 102:25–27, which begins, **"You, O Lord, in the beginning founded the earth, and the heavens are the works of Your hands. They will perish, but You Yourself remain on."**

In the Hebrew of the passage, the one addressed is Yahweh, and the citation proclaims the eternity of Yahweh as a witness to His power and His ability to bring in His Kingdom, so that "the children of His servants may dwell securely" (Ps. 102:28). The writer of this epistle, however, applies it to the Messiah, using it to confirm the eternal transcendence of Messiah in contrast to the created nature of the angels; and his readers evidently also understood it to be a reference to Messiah. How can this be? How can the writer of our epistle apply to Messiah a passage which seems not to be messianic at all but simply a statement of God's eternity?

The answer is found in the Greek Septuagint version of this psalm, which the author of the epistle used and which differs somewhat from the Hebrew. The Hebrew of Psalm 102:23–25 reads, "He has weakened my strength in the way; He has shortened my days. I say, 'O my God, do not take me away in the midst of my

II. Christ Superior to the Angels   Hebrews 1:8–12

days; Your years are throughout all generations. Of old You laid the foundation of the earth.'" The Greek of that same passage reads, "He answered Me in the way of His strength, 'Tell Me the shortness of My days; take Me not away in the midst of My days; Your years are throughout all generations. You, Lord, in the beginning laid the foundation of the earth.'"

In the Hebrew of these verses, we have the supplication of a man to God, asking God to save him from an untimely death, and *the entire psalm is in the voice of the suppliant*. In the Greek version of these same verses, we have a very different situation. The suppliant's prayer comes to an end with verse 22, and verses 23 and following (the passage cited above) *constitute God's answer to the suppliant*. The citation begins, "He answered Me," and this must mean that God answered the suppliant.

What then did God answer Him? God answered, "Tell Me the shortness of My days; take Me not away in the midst of My days" (that is, "acknowledge the shortness of my set time to act and to save Zion and do not summon Me when My time is only half gone"). God continues His answer by adding, "You, Lord, in the beginning laid the foundation of the earth."

Who is this suppliant whom God Himself addresses as **Lord**? Who could this be whom God calls the one who **in the beginning founded the earth**? For a reader of the Septuagint, such an exalted Person could only be the Lord Messiah, the One through whom God made the earth. Thus, this passage is recognized as messianic by the author of the epistle because these verses in the Greek constitute part of a dialogue God has with the suppliant, and not (as in the Hebrew) the cry of the suppliant himself.

For the writer of our epistle, this passage also witnesses dramatically to the eternity of the Messiah, in contrast to the heavens—and all the angels they contain. Just as a man outlasts his clothes, so Messiah will outlast the earth. The contrast with the angelic could not be starker. Angels are compared with such ephemeral things as wind and lightning; Messiah is boldly stated to be eternal. Obviously Messiah cannot simply be a kind of angel.

❦ EXCURSUS
On the Use of the Septuagint

The Septuagint (the Greek version of the Old Testament, translated from the Hebrew over the years beginning in the mid-third century BC) has pride of place among the versions in the Orthodox Church. It differs from the received version of the Hebrew text (the so-called "Masoretic text") in a number of places and in some instances represents an arguably older version of the original Hebrew than the Masoretic text from which most English language versions are translated. (We note in passing that other Hebrew versions existed which differed from the Masoretic text, including the so-called "Samaritan Pentateuch.")

Among the translations, the Septuagint was preeminently the Bible of the early Church. Many Fathers knew only this version of it, and its canon determined the Old Testament of the Church (so that, for example, the Church accepted as Scripture such books as Sirach and the Wisdom of Solomon). St. Cyril of Jerusalem echoes the thought of many when he says that the Septuagint possesses an authority not held by other versions and translations. He writes, "The process [of translating the Septuagint from the Hebrew text] was no . . . contrivance of human wisdom. On the contrary, the translation was effected by the Holy Spirit, by whom the Divine Scriptures were spoken" (*Catechetical Lectures*).

Some Fathers were aware that the Greek version differed in certain ways from the original Hebrew. They accounted for this difference by accepting the Hebrew as the divine original and the Greek as the inspired translation and commentary upon it. (We may note that their whole insistence on the basic reliability of the Septuagint was informed by the Jewish-Christian polemics of their day, in which the Jews derided the Septuagint as unreliable and distorting.)

Certainly we must acknowledge a certain preeminence

in the Greek Septuagint. This is not simply because most of the New Testament citations of the Old Testament are from the Septuagint, but also because some of the Greek renderings of the Hebrew text determine the Church's exegesis. Among such renderings we think of the Septuagint rendering of Isaiah 7:14: "Behold, a virgin [Gr. *parthenos*] shall conceive in the womb and bring forth a Son." The Hebrew text says, "Behold, a young woman [Heb. *almah*] shall conceive." While the two renderings are not mutually incompatible (virgins can be young women, and vice versa), we must acknowledge that St. Matthew's understanding of the passage he quotes in 1:23 presupposes the Greek version.

Similarly, the exegesis of Psalm 102:25–27 given by the author of Hebrews in 1:10–12 presupposes the Greek version of the passage. Indeed, as we have shown above, his messianic understanding of the passage vanishes if the Hebrew text is presupposed. The Hebrew text is not to be thrown out and may still function as the fundamental text from which translations are made. But in the Christian translation and exegesis of the text, we must give pride of place to the Septuagint version cited by the apostles and first readers of the New Testament.

꧁ ꧁ ꧁ ꧁ ꧁

13 But to which of the angels has He ever said, "Sit at My right *hand,* until I put your enemies *as* a footstool for your feet"?

14 Are they not all offering spirits, sent out for service on account of those who are about to inherit salvation?

The author has yet another example of the language of sovereignty used to describe the Son. In Psalm 110:1, God spoke to the Messiah, saying, **"Sit at My right *hand,* until I put your enemies *as***

a footstool for your feet." That is, Messiah is to share the authority of God and have all His foes destroyed by the Almighty. Messiah does not simply exercise a limited authority of His own. Rather, God makes Him share His own boundless authority, ruling over all the earth. **To which of the angels has** God **ever** given such a promise? Such language is never used of them. Rather, Scripture always uses the language of servanthood.

By asking **to which of the angels has He ever said** things like these, the author of Hebrews is not requesting a citation. Rather, he is pointing out a difference in essential atmosphere and vocabulary. Whenever Scripture speaks of angels, we find ourselves using the language of the court, which emphasizes the distance of God from His angelic courtiers and servants. This is fundamentally different from the references to Messiah. There the vocabulary has a different feel; it radiates confidence, sovereignty, power. Far from stressing the distance of the Son to the Father, it stresses His nearness. These contrasting vocabularies highlight the essential difference between the Son and the angels.

Our author concludes with the question, **Are not** the angels **all offering spirits** (Gr. *leitourgika pneumata*—literally, "liturgizing spirits," spirits who serve as the levitical priests do when they offer up their worship at the altar)? **All** the angels—even the most exalted of them—are simply such servants and acolytes. They are **sent out** by God to do **service** (Gr. *diakonia*), not just for the Messiah, but also for His human servants the Christians, those who **are about to inherit salvation**. The angels therefore could never be referred to in such exalted terms as he has shown are used to describe the Messiah. Rather, they are servants of the Lord's human servants. Obviously the Lord could not be an angel Himself.

§I.2. Christ's Word Greater than the Law Given through Angels (2:1–4)

2 1 For this *reason* it is necessary for us to pay far

II. Christ Superior to the Angels — Hebrews 2:1-4

> more attention to what we have heard, lest we drift away *from it*.
> 2 For if the word spoken through angels became confirmed, and every transgression and disobedience received a righteous recompense,
> 3 how will we *ourselves* flee-away if we neglect so great a salvation? After it was at first spoken through the Lord, it was confirmed to us by the ones who heard,
> 4 God also co-witnessing *at the same time*, both by signs and wonders and various miracles and distributions of the Holy Spirit according to His own will.

It is because of the superiority of Christ to the angels that **it is necessary for us to pay far more attention to what we have heard, lest we drift away *from it*.** The image used here is that of a boat which gradually **drifts away** from a safe harbor to be wrecked on the rocks. The Hebrew Christians addressed in this epistle were too heedless of their spiritual state and presumed that because they were Jews, they were safe. On the contrary, says the author of our work, their self-confidence in their spiritual safety was misplaced. If they drifted away from their allegiance to Christ, God would treat them as apostates.

This was apparent in a comparison of the old and the new covenants. In the old covenant, which was **spoken through angels**, the **word** given by God **became confirmed** and was unalterable. The penalties prescribed for apostasy were severe and inescapable. If anyone "sinned with a high hand" (Num. 15:30), defiantly repudiating the divine covenant, that person was to be "cut from the people" and killed. **Every** single **transgression and disobedience received a righteous recompense** under this old covenant; there was no mercy for apostates. If apostasy from this covenant received such severe punishment, how much more would apostasy from the new covenant of Christ? How could the readers of the epistle hope to **flee-away** and escape if they were to **neglect so**

great a salvation as Christ provided and fall from loyalty to Him?

To make his point, the author compares the two covenants, showing how immeasurably greater was Christ's covenant than the old covenant—and therefore how much more severely apostasy from it would be treated.

Our author describes the old covenant as the **word spoken through angels**. That is, God gave the Law to Israel through the mediation of the angels. In Deuteronomy 33:2 (LXX), the giving of the Law on Sinai is described thus: "The Lord has come from Sinai . . . with ten thousands of His holy ones; on His right hand were His angels with Him." This is echoed in several New Testament texts, where the Law is described as "ordained by angels" (Acts 7:53; Gal. 3:19). That is, mere men could not bear the direct voice of God but received His words as delivered by others. Just as Moses could see the face of God and live, but only beheld the fading afterglow of His presence (Ex. 33:20–23), so men could not bear His voice either. Therefore, God gave His word and presence to His angels, who bore them to men on Mount Sinai. This does not mean that God Himself was not directly involved, or that He sent His Law to Israel through a kind of angelic delivery service. But it does mean that He was present on Mount Sinai as an epiphany, not in the fullness of His power. His presence there was a mediated presence, not a full disclosure. In this age, He is still a God who hides Himself (Is. 45:15), since men cannot endure His unveiled presence.

Such a covenant is glorious enough, but the later new covenant of Christ was more glorious still. The word was **spoken through the Lord** Himself, not just delivered through His angels. It was **confirmed to us**, the generation of Christians living after the first Christian Day of Pentecost, by the apostles, **the ones who** first **heard** the Lord speak when He was alive. More than that, **God also** added His testimony to the divine origin of Jesus' message, **co-witnessing at the same time** as the apostles preached by working **signs and wonders and various miracles** through them, giving them **distributions of the Holy Spirit according to His own will**, generously pouring out upon them such gifts as prophecy, tongues, and supernatural knowledge. The presence of such supernatural manifestations in the

Church is a clear testimony to the divine origin of the Gospel. The Law was given through angels, the Gospel by the Lord Himself. To retreat from such an obviously divine message and salvation is obviously to invite the wrath of God.

§I.3. Christ Made Lower than the Angels to Suffer Death as High-Priest (2:5–18)

> ॐ ॐ ॐ ॐ ॐ
>
> 5 For not to angels did He submit the world, about which we are speaking.
> 6 But someone somewhere has testified, saying, "What is man, that You remember him? Or the son of man, that You look at him?
> 7 "You have made him for a little *while* lesser than the angels; You have crowned him with glory and honor;
> 8 "You have put all things in submission under his feet." For in submitting all things to him, He left nothing that is insubordinate to him. But now we do not yet see all things submitted to him.
> 9 But we see Jesus, who was made for a little *while* lesser than the angels, because of the suffering of death crowned with glory and honor, so that by the grace of God He might taste death for everyone.

Having established that Christ is greater than the angels (and therefore that His covenant is greater than the Law, which was ordained through the angels), the author goes on to explain how it is that Christ was made lower than the angels. For if Christ was indeed greater than the angels, how could it be that He suffered a humiliating death?

The author begins his argument by asserting that **the world** to come is **submitted** to Jesus precisely because He *is* lower than the angels—that is, because He is true man. For in the Scripture, it is revealed that **the world** with all its authorities (Gr. *oikoumene*; compare its use in 1:6) was submitted to *man*, **not to** the **angels**. **Someone testified** and made this solemn challenge **somewhere** in the Scriptures (in Ps. 8:4–6 LXX) about the dignity of man: "**What is man, that you look at Him** with mercy? **You have made him for a little *while* lesser than the angels; You have crowned him with glory and honor; You have put all things in submission under his feet.**" (The exact location of this citation is left as the unspecified voice of **someone somewhere**, since what matters for the author of our epistle is that this is Scripture, the voice of God.)

In its original context, this psalm was a meditation on the awe-inspiring privilege bestowed on mankind by God—that men should share the divine authority on earth, being made only a little lesser than God in heaven Himself. In the Hebrew of this text, man is said to be less than *Elohim*, the usual Hebrew word for God. The Hebrew word is, however, actually in the plural, "gods," and the Septuagint translates it as *aggelous*, **the angels**. In its original context of Psalm 8, the difference is not that significant, for the main point remains: that man on earth is only somewhat less than those in heaven.

For the author of our epistle, however, this different reading is important and crucial, for it allows him to assert that Jesus was indeed made not only less than God, but even **lesser than the angels**, since He was true man. Not only that, as the Second Adam, He was the true Head of the human race. God had promised in Genesis 1:28 that all the world would be subject to man, and that man would rule as God's vice-regent over all. This promise was reaffirmed in Psalm 8, and the author of our epistle affirms that it is fulfilled in Jesus. In Jesus, man reaches his true and original destiny and exercises all the authority over the earth that was his at first.

Thus Psalm 8 is not only about man in general, as a race; it is also about Jesus in particular. He is the messianic Son of Man in whom the human race finds its true and perfect expression. The psalmist affirms that **man** is to be **crowned with glory and honor**, and this destiny is fulfilled in the heavenly glory and honor of Jesus. Jesus

II. Christ Superior to the Angels — Hebrews 2:5–9

rules from heaven over all, with **all things in submission under His feet**, and He reigns as glorified man. The author of the epistle stresses that this authority is complete—**in submitting all things to man** (that is, to Jesus), God **left nothing that is insubordinate to Him** and outside His authority. That is, the angels also are submitted to Jesus. It is not that Jesus is now equal with the angels. The Scripture cited proves that **all things** are submitted to Jesus—not excepting the angels.

Nonetheless, the author also admits that **now we do not yet see all things submitted to him**. That is, in this present age, man's sovereignty and glory are not seen and have not yet been vindicated. Many things still hold man in thrall and in fear—not just things like wild animals and the untamable forces of nature, but, most importantly, death itself. In the same way, the authority and glory and honor of Jesus, the Head of the human race and its King and representative, also are not seen. When Jesus walked the earth as man, He partook of our humility and powerlessness, being subject to weakness and death, just as we are. **Now**, in this age, we **do not see all things submitted** to Jesus, **but we see Jesus for a little *while* lesser than the angels**.

His humility and His status as lower than the angels should not therefore be a stumbling block. The Messiah is indeed to be more glorious than the angels and to be exalted above all. As true man, Jesus will be so. But He had to be **made for a little *while* lesser than the angels** in order to experience the **suffering of death** for our sake, **so that by the grace of God He might taste death for everyone**. For if He continued to exist in a state superior to the angels, He could not have undergone the bitterness of death that only human beings experience. The Incarnation, whereby the Son became mortal man for our sake, and thus lower than the angels, was necessary for our salvation. But this lower state was but a temporary prelude to His future messianic exaltation, when He would be **crowned with glory and honor** as God's reward for His humility, and take His seat at the Father's right hand as the true Son of Man foretold in Psalm 8.

> ༄ ༄ ༄ ༄ ༄
> 10 For it was proper for Him, for whom are all things and through whom are all things, in bringing many sons to glory, to perfect the Leader of their salvation through sufferings.

It was only **proper for** God the Father, **for whom are all things and through whom are all things**, to make His divine Son lesser than the angels. The Father was sovereign over all His creation and could make all things serve His purposes—even the humiliation of Christ. It was not unworthy for God to **perfect** the Messiah and to have Him reach His final goal **through sufferings**, even if some Jews thought it was unbecoming of Messiah to suffer. On the contrary, it was most fitting. Messiah was the **Leader** (Gr. *archegos*) **of** men's **salvation**, the One who blazed the path. (The Greek word means not only a founder, but also someone who is the first in a series and who supplies the impetus.) His **many sons** who must also be brought **to glory** must themselves travel through suffering, and so their **Leader** must travel that way as well. How else could they find their way?

A word may be said about the notion of Jesus being **perfected**. The English word has a moral feel to it; one who is not yet perfect is therefore imperfect and morally defective. The Greek word used (*teleioo*) has no such connotation. It is cognate with the word *telos*, "end, goal," and here it simply means that Jesus reached His appointed goal through suffering.

> ༄ ༄ ༄ ༄ ༄
> 11 For both He who sanctifies and those who are sanctified are all from one; for which cause He is not ashamed *at all* to call them brothers,
> 12 saying, "I will declare Your Name to my brothers, and in the midst of the church I will *sing* hymns to You."
> 13 And again, "I *myself* will put my confidence

II. Christ Superior to the Angels   Hebrews 2:11–13

> in Him," and again, "Behold, I *myself* and the children whom God has given me."

This is also said to be proper because **both He who sanctifies** (that is, Jesus) **and those who are sanctified** (that is, the Christians) **are all from one** source, the Father. Jesus looks to the Father as to His coeternal Source, and we Christians also look to the Father as the Monarch of all.

The author once again characteristically makes his point by citing a series of Scriptures. In Psalm 22:22, the Psalmist says, **"I will declare Your Name to my brothers, and in the midst of the church I will *sing* hymns to You."** This psalm was acknowledged to be messianic. Not only did it prophesy of Christ's sufferings (beginning with His cry from the Cross, "My God, my God, why have You forsaken me?" and speaking of His being "pierced" and of lots being cast for His garments), it also speaks of the time when "all the earth would remember and turn to the Lord." In the verse cited by our author, the messianic voice of the psalmist speaks of **declaring** God's **Name** and His mighty works **to his brothers**, the other children of Israel. The messianic psalmist would *sing* hymns to God as part of a mighty throng of fellow-worshippers, **in the midst of the church** (Gr. *ekklesia*), the solemn assembly for worship. Thus, the Messiah is portrayed as part of the people of Israel, in full solidarity with the children of men. This proves that the incarnate Christ has one and the same source as we do (the Father) and that He was to be made lesser than the angels, as we are.

The author brings forward two other Scriptures as well, from Isaiah 8:17, **"I *myself* will put my confidence in Him,"** and the verse following it, **"Behold, I *myself* and the children whom God has given me."** Once again, the Greek Septuagint version of these verses differs somewhat from the Hebrew, for in the Greek these verses are prefaced by the words, "And one will say," so that verses 17 and 18 constitute what this person will say. Given that these verses form part of an extended Emmanuel prophecy (preceded by the prophecy of the virgin conceiving in 7:14 and followed by the prophecy of the Child being born in 9:6), it is natural to infer that the "one" who will speak about being "a sign and wonder in Israel" (the conclusion of 8:18) is the Messiah.

According to this understanding, it is the Messiah who says that He **will put** His **confidence** in God, trusting Him and waiting for God to vindicate Him. For the author of our epistle, this shows how the Messiah shares our nature, for Messiah is in the position of waiting on God also. Messiah is in solidarity with us, and He also looks to God for help.

This is revealed in the next part of the Isaiah passage quoted. The Messiah is here understood as talking about **the children** which **God has given** Him. These **children** are His disciples. By referring to the disciples of Jesus as His **children**, the prophecy here again reveals that both Messiah and His disciples share the same nature.

For the author of our epistle, therefore, the Scriptures clearly present the Messiah as sharing our nature, being made lesser than the angels, even as we are.

༄ ༄ ༄ ༄ ༄

14 Since therefore the children share in flesh and blood, He Himself likewise also partook of the same, that through death He might nullify him who had death's might, that is, the devil,

15 and might release those who through fear of death were liable to slavery all their lives.

16 For surely He does not take hold of angels, but He takes hold of the seed of Abraham.

17 For which reason He was obligated to be made like His brothers in all things, that He might become a merciful and faithful high-priest in things concerning God, to make propitiation for the sins of the people.

18 For because He Himself was tested in that which He has suffered, He is able to help those who are tested.

II. Christ Superior to the Angels   Hebrews 2:14–18

The author then goes on to explain at greater length *why* Messiah was made lesser than the angels. Messiah's disciples or **children** (v. 13) **share in flesh and blood**, all of us living a life of weakness and mortality. Therefore, in order to slay death, He had to **likewise also partake of the same** nature, for only by becoming incarnate in our flesh and blood could He experience death.

This was necessary, for it was **through death** that Christ would **nullify him who had death's might** and power, **that is, the devil**. As the Church sings in her Paschal troparion, Christ trampled down death by death. Only thus could He render the Enemy powerless and **release** all of us, **who through fear of death were liable to slavery all** our **lives**. Prior to Christ's coming, death held all our race in its power, and all cowered in fear before its inevitability. But no more—Christ has now abolished death and set us slaves free, making us into His sons and freedmen.

This is why He had to be made lower than the angels and to suffer death in humility and apparent defeat. **For surely** Christ **does not take hold of angels**, seizing them by the hand and lifting them up from the pit. Rather, He takes hold of the seed of Abraham, rescuing human beings. If He had come to save the angels, He would not have needed to become incarnate or to become lesser than the angels. But in fact He did not come to save the angels but to save us, and therefore He was **obligated** to take on our human nature and be made lower than the angels, being **made like** us **His brothers in all things**.

For this was the essence of high-priesthood. The Jewish high-priest was one in solidarity with those for whom he offered sacrifices. In the same way, if Jesus was to be our **merciful and faithful high-priest in things concerning God** (that is, in the matter of making atonement and in **making propitiation for the sins of the people**), He also must be in solidarity with us, sharing our nature and our life. Indeed, it was only because He experienced all facets of our life—enduring the humility, the suffering, the fear—and was thus **tested in that which He suffered** that He is able to be our Savior at all. It is because He has experienced our lot that **He is able to help those who are tested**. He knows what it is to suffer, and so

He can guide and strengthen those who suffer. As the Fathers said, only that which is assumed is healed. Christ assumed and took upon Himself all our human nature, and so all our human nature can experience His healing.

⊱ III ⊰

CHRIST OUR HIGH-PRIEST
(3:1—10:18)

The main body of the author's argument now begins, extending from here to 10:18. He will argue that Christ is our great and heavenly high-priest and that He is worth the possible sacrifice of his readers' standing in Judaism. Continued loyalty to Christ may cost the Hebrew Christians their standing in the Jewish community and possibly even access to the Temple sacrifices. But they must persevere in their worship of Christ anyway, for in Him they have a high-priest superior to the one functioning in Jerusalem, and the sacrifice of Christ they receive in their weekly Eucharists is infinitely more effective than any sacrifices offered in the Temple. Let them not abandon the immortal divine high-priest for the mortal human ones, nor the effective substance for the prophetic shadows.

§III.1. Christ Greater than Moses (3:1–6)

3 1 For which reason, holy brothers, partakers of a heavenly calling, consider Jesus, the apostle and high-priest of our confession,
2 who was faithful to Him who made Him *high-priest*, as Moses also was in all His house.
3 For this One has been counted worthy of more glory than Moses by so much *more* as he who built the house has more honor than the house.
4 For every house is built by someone, but the one who built all *things* is God.

> 5 Now Moses *was* faithful in His whole house as an attendant, for a witness of the things which were to be spoken *later*;
> 6 but Christ *was faithful* as a Son over His house, whose house we *ourselves* are, if indeed we hold fast the boldness and the boast of the hope.

Because He had come down and been made like us in all things (2:17), our author tells his readers to **consider Jesus** who had been sent from God to be His **apostle** and ambassador, bringing the Father's Word to men, and to be His **high-priest**. That is, they are bidden to focus their attention on Jesus, whom they had acknowledged in their baptismal **confession** of faith, because they were in danger of overlooking His centrality and importance to their salvation. The author addresses the recipients of the epistle as his **holy brothers**. That is, they were holy, for through the Incarnation, they had become **holy** and the **brothers** of Christ Himself (compare 2:17), for through their baptism they had become **partakers of a heavenly calling**. In baptism, God had called them to be His family and to share the sonship of the Son of God in heaven.

As pressure from their Jewish countrymen increased, the readers of the epistle were in danger of forgetting the place Jesus had in the divine dispensation. The author of our epistle therefore reminds them of Christ's superiority over Moses—and therefore of the superiority of their Christian allegiance over their ancestral Judaism.

Moses was indeed important. He was **faithful** to God **in all His house**, fulfilling all that God appointed for him to do. However, he was **faithful as an attendant**, as a mere servant. (The Greek word translated *attendant* here is *therapon*, meaning someone who waits upon another; compare the use of its cognate verb in Acts 17:25.) Moreover, Moses' service was not an end in itself; it was meant **for a witness of the things which were to be spoken** *later*, a type and prophecy of the gospel work of Jesus.

Thus Moses was inferior to Christ. If Moses was a mere attendant in God's household, Christ had the status of a **Son** and an heir to all that house. Furthermore, Christ was not merely set **in** God's house

III. Christ Our High Priest — Hebrews 3:1–6

as Moses was; He was set **over** it as one who had authority. Christ was faithful to God and fulfilled all that God called Him to do, even as Moses did. But Christ had a superior role and greater glory than Moses. He was as superior to Moses as a master is to his slave.

Jewish believers might have thought Moses was the founder of their religion (compare the Pharisees counting themselves as disciples of Moses in John 9:28), but our author reminds his readers that God is the ultimate Founder of their faith, and Moses was simply a part of what God had built. Moses' status remains that of a servant in that divine household—the glory goes not to him but to **God**, for He is **the one who built all *things***. And, because Jesus is the exact representation of God's nature (1:3), Jesus shares that divine glory, so that **this One** (Jesus) **has been counted worthy of more glory than Moses by so much *more* as he who built the house has more honor than the house** itself.

What was the status of the readers? They themselves, as disciples of Jesus (the pronoun *we* is emphatic in the Greek), had become that **house** over which the Son had been set and in which Moses served, and were the very household and family of God. That presupposed their perseverance, of course (the theme of the epistle and the author's reason for writing). They would remain God's **house** if they would but **hold fast the boldness** they had with God as His obedient sons and cling to their Christian Faith, if they would but retain their **boast** to be inheritors of God's Kingdom, which was their secure **hope** in Christ. To be good Jews was not enough; they needed to hold firm as good disciples of Jesus.

In asserting that Christ was superior to Moses, our author makes a bold claim. For Christians today, such an assertion seems self-evident, but that is only because we are the heirs of the Church's conciliar teachings—and because we are not first-century Jews. For the Jews of that time, Moses was a figure of almost superhuman proportions. Moses was credited with learning arithmetic, geometry, astronomy, medicine, and music in Egypt, and with inventing boats and engines for building and for war. He was thought to have taught the Greek Orpheus and the Egyptian Hermes. Some believed he made war upon Egypt's enemies, so that the city of Hermopolis was founded to commemorate his victory. It was with a simple word of his mouth that he slew the Egyptian who attacked an Israelite.

In claiming to be disciples of Moses (John 9:28), the Jews of Jesus' day believed they were submitting themselves to the highest human being who ever lived. The claim that Christ's glory infinitely surpassed that of Moses therefore ran contrary to this basic Jewish impulse. The Law was, for them, the pinnacle of God's revelation to the world, and Moses, as the Lawgiver, stood upon that very pinnacle. Our author here asserts that Christ commands an eminent height far above anything previously known, and that His authority utterly eclipses the loftiest authority they had known before.

§III.2. Beware Lest You Fall Away from Christ's Sabbath Rest (3:7—4:13)

> ৯৯ ৯৯ ৯৯ ৯৯ ৯৯
>
> 7 Therefore just as the Holy Spirit says, "Today if you hear His voice,
> 8 "do not harden your hearts as in the embitterment, in the day of testing in the wilderness,
> 9 "where your fathers tested by proving Me and saw My works for forty years.
> 10 "Therefore I was offended with this generation and said, 'Always they are deceived in their heart, and they did not know My ways';
> 11 "as I swore in My wrath, 'They will not enter into My rest.'"
> 12 Watch out, brothers, lest there should be in any one of you an evil heart of unbelief in withdrawing from the living God.
> 13 But encourage yourselves, each and every day, as long as it is called "today," lest any one of you be hardened by the deceitfulness of sin.

Because their reward depended upon their perseverance, the author exhorts them to **watch out** lest they drift away from their

III. Christ Our High Priest   Hebrews 3:7–13

hope and **withdraw from the living God** of Israel (v. 12)—that is, from their Christian faith. They might be tempted to think they still had faith in the living God as long as they remained good Jews. But our author asserts that to fall away from allegiance to Jesus is to fall away from God and to have a heart full of unbelief. They must not let that **evil heart of unbelief** grow within them. Such a cancer had already begun to grow in some of them, who were forsaking the common Christian assembly on Sundays (10:25). Let all of them beware this dreadful possibility!

To exhort them, he tells them to **encourage** one another, **each and every day**. They were not to exist in isolation from their Christian brethren, living in hermetically sealed compartments, indifferent to the struggles and falls of their friends. Rather they were to look out for one another and urge each other not to **be hardened by the deceitfulness of sin**. Sin might whisper in their ears that defection from Jesus would have no eternal consequences, but this was a lie, a deception. They must be on the lookout for such lies and refuse to hear them.

How were they to give this encouragement? By attendance at the Sunday Eucharist, the weekly Christian assembly. Not only would the customary stories about Jesus encourage them (such oral stories as would later be assembled and preserved in the Gospels), but exhortations from the Christian teachers and elders would provide the much-needed support also. Further, the simple fact of assembling was an invaluable encouragement to one's brethren. One's mere presence spoke volumes to the others who came.

As his own encouragement to perseverance, in good Jewish fashion, our author brings forward a Scripture, Psalm 95:7–11 (in the Greek Septuagint version). As part of Scripture, it was the authentic voice of **the Holy Spirit**, and therefore had prophetic relevance for them now in their struggle as Christians.

The psalm was written as an ancient encouragement for Israel to obey God when they would **hear His voice** in their Law, and **not** to **harden** their **hearts** as Israel did of old. For in the days of Moses, Israel did indeed harden their hearts to God, in the time described as **the embitterment** (Gr. *parapikrasmos*; compare the word *pikros*,

49

"bitter"). During that time in the wilderness before coming into their **rest** in the Promised Land, Israel rebelled against God by **testing** Him and **proving** Him. They refused to trust God, but put Him to the test by demanding water in the desert, not expecting it and ready to stone Moses and return to Egypt (Ex. 17:1–7). And this was not the only occasion of their revolt. Later still in their journeying they were prepared to repudiate their salvation and return to Egypt owing to the lack of water (Num. 20:1–13).

Thus it was that God was **offended with** that **generation** and angrily embittered against them. He had shown them His care, His miraculous **works for forty years**, and still they rebelled against His love. The psalmist presents God as declaring that **always** Israel was **deceived** and led astray from their very **heart** and that **they did not know** or understand His **ways**. Therefore, the psalmist says, **God swore in** His **wrath** that Israel would **not enter into** His **rest**. They would not know refreshment in the Promised Land but would die in the wilderness.

> ॐ ॐ ॐ ॐ ॐ
>
> 14 For we have become partakers of Christ, if indeed we hold fast the beginning of our conviction firm until the end,
> 15 while it is said, "Today if you hear His voice, do not harden your hearts, as in the embitterment."
> 16 For who heard and *yet* embittered *Him*? Indeed, did not all those who came out from Egypt through Moses?
> 17 And with whom was He offended for forty years? Was it not with those who sinned, whose corpses fell in the wilderness?
> 18 And to whom did He swear that they should not enter into His rest, but to those who disobeyed?
> 19 And we see that they were not able to enter because of unbelief.

III. Christ Our High Priest — Hebrews 3:14–19

Building on this Scripture, the author of our epistle applies it to his readers' situation. His readers were saved, for they had **become partakers of Christ** through their baptism. But they must also **hold fast the beginning of** their **conviction firm until the end**, otherwise they would not be partakers of Christ and His salvation at the Last Day. They must not retreat from their allegiance to Jesus and slip back into mere Judaism. The sound of the psalmist, reverberating in their ears and saying to them, **"Today if you hear His voice, do not harden your hearts,"** calls them to constancy.

For their situation was the same as that of the Israelites liberated from Egypt, the ones referred to in Psalm 95. These Israelites, of all Israelites, were truly God's People, the primordial paradigm of Jewish redemption: they had been freed from Pharaoh, and their experience of salvation formed the pattern for all subsequent salvation in Israel. And yet merely making a beginning in this way was not enough for them. They too needed to hold fast their conviction and allegiance to Yahweh firm until the end—and yet they did not do so.

For who heard God's voice at Sinai **and yet** still **embittered *Him*** by their rebellion? **Indeed, did not all those who came out from Egypt through Moses**, the very ones who had been saved—and saved so gloriously as to become the archetypes of salvation? So it is proved that being saved is not enough—one must also persevere. For **with whom was He offended for forty years? Was it not with those who sinned**, those who rebelled against God by turning away from Him? Being saved once was therefore not enough—must one persevere in faith, for the sin of apostasy will bring the judgment of God. So it is proved that if we sin against God and turn away from Christ, God will be offended with us too, and as ***the*** **corpses** of that previous generation **fell in the wilderness**, so God's wrath will be on us as well. And **to whom did *God* swear that they should not enter into His rest, but to those who disobeyed?** So it is proved and **we** can **see** that **they were not able to enter because of** their **unbelief**. If the readers imitate these Israelites in their unbelief by turning from Christ, they too will not be able to enter God's final rest.

> ꙮ ꙮ ꙮ ꙮ ꙮ
>
> **4** 1 Therefore let us be afraid lest, while a promise is left open of entering into His rest, any one of you should seem to have lacked.
> 2 For indeed we have had *good news* preached to us, just as they also; but the word they heard did not profit those ones, because it was not blended with faith in those who heard.
> 3 For we who have believed enter into that rest, just as He has said, "As I swore in My wrath, they will not enter into My rest," although His works were *there* from the foundation of the world.
> 4 For He has thus said somewhere about the seventh *day*, "And God rested on the seventh day from all His works";
> 5 and again in this *Scripture*, "They will not enter into My rest."

The author continues with his exhortation from Psalm 95. The result of God's word in that psalm is that **a promise** to us is **left open of entering into His rest**. That is, God had spoken through David to encourage Israel to enter His rest through their faithful obedience, and the readers of the epistle should **be afraid** and take care to obey, lest any of them should finally **lack** that rest. There was no reason for them to **lack** it—the way had been **left open** by God and His promise remained to be claimed.

Indeed, they **had *good news* preached** to them, **just as** the Israelites of old **also** did. The Israelites, however, failed because **the word they heard** was **not blended with faith**. They heard God's Word on Mount Sinai but did not internalize it, **blending** it with inner **faith** so that His Word lived in their hearts. The readers of the epistle, like the Israelites of old, also had *good news* preached to them (the verb is *euaggelizo*, cognate with *euaggelion*, "Gospel").

In the case of the Israelites, the good news was the call of Yahweh to be His people, a kingdom of priests, a holy nation (Ex. 19:6); in the case of the epistle's readers, the good news was the call of Christ to follow Him and inherit the Kingdom. Though the content of the good news differed, both groups had been called into covenant with God and were called to salvation. The readers of the epistle must take care to receive the calling with faith, and so **profit** from it and enter God's rest in the Kingdom.

If they would continue to **believe** and persevere in that faith, they would indeed finally **enter into that rest**. Here the author describes the nature of that rest, using a classical Jewish method of interpretation (the so-called *Midrashic* method), digging into the individual words of a text to discover a deeper meaning. The passage in Psalm 95 had spoken about the unbelieving Israelites **not entering into** God's **rest**. Our author examines the word *rest* to discover what exactly this rest was, and he says it was none other than the Sabbath rest which God took after the six days of creation. For it is **said somewhere** in the Scripture (Gen. 2:2; see 2:6 note) that **God rested on the seventh day from all His works**. Obviously, our author concludes, the **rest** of God mentioned in Psalm 95:11 (**they will not enter into My rest**) was a sharing in this primordial and eternal rest with God, when He rested from His works and invited man to join Him in unbroken fellowship. The unbelieving Israelites had no excuse for not entering God's rest, since it was available from the **foundation of the world**. All they needed to do was believe and serve God with obedient faith.

> ꙮ ꙮ ꙮ ꙮ ꙮ
>
> 6 Since therefore it is left for some to enter into it, and those who at first had *good news* preached *to them* did not enter because of disobedience,
> 7 He again appointed a certain day, "Today," saying through David after so long a time just as has been said-before, "Today if you hear His voice, do not harden your hearts."
> 8 For if Joshua had *given* them rest, He would

> not have spoken after that about another day.
> 9 So there is left a Sabbath-keeping for the people of God.
> 10 For the one who has entered into His rest has himself also rested from his works, as God *did* from His own *works*.

Our author continues to examine his text from Psalm 95. God willed that His people **enter into** rest with Him, and this opportunity is **left** for any who would avail themselves of it. The Israelites in the time of Moses and Joshua, **those who at first had *good news* preached *to them*, did not enter** His rest, but fell in the wilderness and did not enter the Promised Land (Deut. 1:34–35). But God still strove to call His people to rest and fellowship with Him, and so again, in the time of **David** (who wrote Psalm 95; the Davidic authorship is found in the Septuagint version, though not in the Masoretic Hebrew), **after so long a time** from Moses and Joshua, **again appointed a certain day** to enter His rest. That day was **today,** for David had written (as the author of our epistle **said-before** in the previous chapter), **"Today if you hear His voice, do not harden your hearts."** That is, God, through David, was still calling His people to faith and to rest with Him.

Some interpreters may have thought "rest" in Psalm 95 referred not to eternal rest with God (such as the Christians will enjoy at their life's end in the Kingdom), but only to temporal rest in Canaan. Indeed, in the context of Psalm 95, when God swears that unbelieving Israel "will not enter [His] rest," this historically meant they would not enter the Promised Land but would die in the wilderness.

The author of our epistle, however, defends his view that a deeper and more eternal interpretation of this "rest" is intended. Its meaning *cannot* have been exhausted by reference to entry into Canaan. The Psalmist *cannot* have meant that when God said "they will never enter into My rest," He meant only that they would not enter the Promised Land. For, our author argues, Israel *did* enter the Promised Land under Joshua. If by "rest" the Psalmist meant entry into the land of Canaan and nothing more, he would not have

III. Christ Our High Priest — Hebrews 4:11–13

challenged Israel to enter that rest. If the **rest** the Psalmist meant were the historical one **Joshua had *given* them**, the Psalmist **would not have spoken after that** time **about another day** and another rest. By challenging Israel in the time of David to enter God's rest, the Psalmist *clearly presupposed that Israel had not yet done it.* Thus the "rest" referred to in Psalm 95 could *not* have meant the rest of entry into Canaan under Joshua, but the eternal rest of fellowship with God, which had been available to all the faithful from the foundation of the world. The "rest" of entering into Canaan thus had a profounder meaning than the merely historical note. It was, even in David's time, to carry the freight of a more timeless rest and peace with God.

So, our author concludes, **there is left** available to his readers, as **the people of God**, a spiritual **Sabbath-keeping** (Gr. *sabbatismos*, cognate with *sabbatizo*, "to keep the Sabbath"). That is, they are called to persevere in their belief in Christ and thus **enter into** God's **rest** at the end of their lives, when they will have **rested from** their **works**, even **as God *did* from His own *works*** at the beginning of creation. For the Jews, the Sabbath was the heart of their religion and a time of joy and fellowship with God. Here is the true meaning of that Sabbath, our author says, and the Sabbath's consummation—rest and fellowship with God forever after a life of faithful works. Let his readers cling to their faith and enjoy this final and eternal Sabbath-keeping to which they were called. (We may note in passing that the author here is referring to keeping the Sabbath rest in the age to come, not to a liturgical Sabbath-keeping on the seventh day of each week. Even in the first century, Christian Jews met for their weekly synaxis and Eucharist on the first day of the week.)

> ༄ ༄ ༄ ༄ ༄
>
> 11 Therefore let us be diligent to enter into that rest, lest anyone fall through the same example of disobedience.
> 12 For the Word of God *is* living and working and sharper than any two-edged sword, and penetrating as far as the division of soul and

> spirit, of both joints and marrow, and *able* to discern the thoughts and insights of the heart. 13 And there is no creature unmanifest before Him, but all things *are* naked and helpless to the eyes of Him to whom our account *will be given.*

He concludes his exhortation with a warning. They must **be diligent** in their faith if they would **enter into that rest**. The word translated *be diligent* is the Greek *spoudazo*, sometimes rendered "be eager, zealous, earnest, take pains with." If the Hebrew readers were to enter God's rest, they must not simply coast along but make strenuous efforts and keep their fire burning brightly. If they withdrew from Jesus and from the living God (3:12), they would **fall**, even as the Israelites fell in the wilderness (3:17), since they indulged in **the same example of disobedience** as they.

They therefore must not trifle with God. **The Word of God**, the Gospel to which they responded, was no idle message. It was **living** and would judge any who disdained it; it was **working** and effective in its power to condemn any who rejected it; it was **sharper than any two-edged sword**. As such a sharp sword could pierce the human body through to its very core, so also the Gospel message could **penetrate as far as the division of soul and spirit, of both joints and marrow**; it was *able* **to discern the thoughts and insights of the heart.**

That is, God would one day judge all through and through, bringing into His scrutiny not only one's actions, but also one's secret motivations and intentions. Every nook and cranny of one's secret **heart**, all the subconscious springs of action, would be subject to God's gaze and judgment. Indeed, there was **no creature** living who was **unmanifest** or hidden **before Him**. **All things** were **naked and helpless** to His **eyes**—to **Him to whom** the **account** for our secret sins must one day be given. (The word rendered *helpless* is the passive of the Greek *trachelizo*, "to grab around the throat"; the image is of someone caught by a wrestler around the throat and thus rendered helpless. There will be no escape from God!) Thus, if anyone withdrew from loyalty to Christ, walking in **disobedience**, that one would surely **fall**. There would be no exceptions. The Gospel would judge all who willfully rejected it.

§III.3. Christ Our High-Priest (4:14—5:10)

> 🙢 🙢 🙢 🙢 🙢
>
> 14 Therefore, having a great high-priest who has gone through the heavens, Jesus the Son of God, let us hold onto our confession.
> 15 For we do not have a high-priest who is unable to sympathize with our weaknesses, but One who has been tested in all things as *we are*, yet without sin.
> 16 Therefore let us with boldness come near to the throne of grace, that we may receive mercy and may find grace for timely help.

Having spoken of Christ's superiority to Moses and of the necessity of persevering in order to enter true Sabbath rest, the author of the epistle then begins to explain in greater depth how Christ is his readers' high-priest. His high-priesthood was important, for Christ was in fact all they needed, and the priesthood and sacrifices in Jerusalem were actually irrelevant to their salvation.

He begins by exhorting them to **hold onto** their **confession** of Jesus as the Messiah and their Christian Faith. The word translated *hold onto* is the Greek *krateo*, sometimes translated "seize"; it is used for the soldiers seizing and arresting Jesus in Mark 14:44. The readers therefore were exhorted to keep a tight grip on their Faith. This was fitting, because that Faith was precious. Jesus was not just their high-priest, but their **great high-priest**, for He had **gone through the heavens** to sit at the right hand of God. The reference to Christ going through the heavens stresses His present transcendence and universal sovereignty. He now abides far above our world with its mortality, sin, and weakness (compare 7:26). But His removal to a place far above did not mean that He was now **unable to sympathize**

with their **weaknesses** or that their present sufferings and persecution were of no concern to Him. On the contrary, He too had been persecuted and had suffered; He **had been tested in all things as** His followers were, **yet without sin**. He had emerged triumphant from His sufferings and had not given in to the temptation to veer from His course.

The Greek word rendered here as *test* is *peirazo*, meaning "to make trial of, to tempt, to put to the test." It involves not just a temptation to sin but any form of testing or trial. In Wisdom 3:5 it is used of the trials and sufferings of the righteous. Its predominant meaning here is that of being tested by suffering—though of course the meaning of being tempted to sin as a way out of that suffering is not entirely absent either.

Because of Christ's experience of being tried, He is able to help His servants when they suffer. They must therefore **with boldness come near to the throne of grace**. That is, they must come week by week to the Eucharist and as a body ask Christ for His help. (This does not mean, of course, that they may not pray for that help individually, apart from the church assembly, also.) For Christ's **throne** is one **of grace**—He is always willing to graciously use His power to save His own and to give them **mercy** and **grace for timely help**. In the hour of crisis, they could be sure of His heavenly aid. For giving such help to the weak is what high-priests do (5:1).

In describing the necessity of **coming near with boldness to the throne of grace**, our author reveals an essential characteristic of Christian worship—that of access with boldness. The word rendered here *boldness* is the Greek *parresia*, denoting a freedom of speech, a confidence of being accepted, "permission to speak freely" (as soldiers sometimes say).

In our age of easy democracy, we take it for granted that any and all should have access to the rulers of the land. It was not so in ancient times. In Persia, for example, no one could approach the throne unbidden, and to do so could mean death (see Esther 4:11). In a similar way, sinful man cannot stand before God nor speak with easy familiarity. Isaiah had a vision of the holy God and knew that he was ruined, for he was a man of unclean lips, dwelling in the midst

III. Christ Our High Priest — Hebrews 5:1–4

of a people of unclean lips, and he had seen the King, the Lord of Hosts. It was only when God cleansed his lips that he could speak to God—and for Him (see Is. 6). So also with us. Of ourselves, we dare not approach the holy God. Only through Christ, our great High Priest, do we find the cleansing and boldness to approach His throne.

Our Christian liturgical assemblies, based on divinely given *parresia*, constitute our approach to His throne to **receive mercy** and to **find grace**. Through our worship—the hymns, the prayers, the readings of Scripture, and especially in the reception of the Eucharistic Mysteries—we are filled with mercy and grace. Christian worship is thus an encounter with the living God, an encounter that leaves us transformed. We come empty and leave full; we come in need of mercy and leave pardoned; we come helpless and leave overflowing with God's favor and strength. The Jewish Christians of the first century needed such strength to persevere in the face of the trials from their fellow Jews. We also need that strength as we face the challenges besetting us today.

> **5** 1 For every high-priest taken from men is appointed for men in things concerning God, that he may offer up both gifts and sacrifices for sins;
> 2 he is able to deal gently with the ignorant and deceived, since he himself also is surrounded with weakness;
> 3 and because of it he is obligated to offer *sacrifices* for sins, as for the people, thus also for himself.
> 4 And no one takes the honor to himself, but is called by God, even as Aaron also *was*.

Our author continues to show how Christ is our true high-priest by examining the characteristics of all Jewish high-priests and showing how these are found in Christ.

First of all, **every high-priest taken from men** on earth (as in Judaism) **is appointed** by God **for men in things concerning God**. That is, the high-priest's primary function is to bring men to God, and he does that by **offering up both** votive **gifts** (as expressions of gratitude) **and** also **sacrifices for sins**. The high-priest **is able to deal gently with the ignorant and deceived**—that is, those who sinned in ignorance, succumbing to moral weakness and not intending to reject all of God's covenant (compare Num. 15:28–31). He can do this because **he himself also is surrounded** and beset **with** moral **weakness**; he knows that it is the common lot of men to drink iniquity like water and that a man cannot be pure before His Maker (Job 4:17; 15:16). The high-priest is in solidarity with those for whom he offers sacrifices, and so **he is obligated to offer *sacrifices* for sins, as for the people, thus also for himself** (compare Lev. 16:6), since he also is a sinner. He does not reject them for their sinfulness or haughtily refuse to help them. Rather he **deals gently** with them (Gr. *metriophatheo*, literally "to moderate one's feelings"), softening his heart and restoring them to God.

Secondly, **no one takes the honor** of being high-priest **to himself, but** rather **is called by God** to that task, **even as Aaron** was. Aaron did not decide himself that he wanted to be high-priest, and there was no strife between him and other contenders. Rather, God called him to that task. Aaron's successors in that office also were called by God to that role through their birth, for it was only the sons of Aaron who could be high-priest. If one from another tribe or another family or clan desired the role or tried to buy it, it was no use. God through His providence called one to that office; no element of self-promotion was involved.

To fully appreciate the role of the high-priest and how he is a fitting type of Christ, we need to look at the Old Testament with different eyes than we sometimes use. Of necessity the office of Jewish high-priest vanished with the destruction of the Jewish Temple in AD 70, and we know the office perhaps most intimately from reading about Caiaphas, the high-priest in the time of Jesus. Some Christians today know a bit about Aaron and are familiar with the levitical regulations governing the high-priest. But Aaron is something of a

III. Christ Our High Priest — Hebrews 5:5–10

shadowy figure. The figure of Caiaphas leaps from the pages of the New Testament with greater clarity of detail than the figure of Aaron leaps from the pages of the Old. That is in some ways unfortunate, for Caiaphas was not a worthy bearer of that high office, and his sin can have the effect of clouding the office's true radiance.

To appreciate the office of high-priest, one should read its description in Sirach 50, which describes a more worthy incumbent, the high-priest Simon son of Onias. The author of Sirach describes him as "glorious, surrounded by the people as he came out of the House of the curtain. Like the morning star among the clouds, like the full moon at the festal season, like the sun shining on the Temple of the Most High. . . . When he received the portions from the hands of the priests, he was like a young cedar on Lebanon. . . . Then Simon came down and raised his hands over the whole congregation of Israelites, to pronounce the blessing of the Lord with his lips . . . and they bowed down in worship, to receive the blessing from the Most High" (Sirach 50:5–7, 12, 20–21).

The author of Sirach presents an image of glory, of splendor, of a man mediating the divine presence and blessing by virtue of his office and righteous life. It is in this context that Paul wrote rapturously of "the glory, the covenants, the temple service" (Rom. 9:4). For the Jew, the high-priest imaged the glory of God, and his splendid sacerdotal vestments were but a reflection of the majesty of God, who manifested His presence through the services over which the high-priest presided. Even St. John, while acknowledging the unworthy and sinful character of Caiaphas, admitted that his "prophecy" about the death of Jesus was made by virtue of his high-priestly office (John 11:51). St. John may have had no love for Caiaphas, but he still respected the office he held. The office of high-priest is indeed a worthy type and prefiguring of the Savior.

> ❧ ❧ ❧ ❧ ❧
>
> 5 Thus also Christ did not glorify Himself to become high-priest, but He *appointed Him* who said to Him, "You *Yourself* are My Son, today I *Myself* have begotten You,"

> 6 just as He says also in another *scripture*, "You *Yourself* are a priest forever, according to the order of Melchizedek."
> 7 In the days of His flesh, He offered up both supplications and pleas to the One able to save Him from death, with strong shouting and tears, and He was heard because of His reverence.
> 8 Although He was *the* Son, He learned obedience from what He suffered.
> 9 And having been made perfect, He became to all who obey Him the source of eternal salvation,
> 10 being designated by God a high-priest according to the order of Melchizedek.

Having listed the characteristics of a high-priest, our author goes on to show how Jesus fit these characteristics exactly. For **Christ did not glorify Himself to become high-priest**, **but** God appointed Him. Jesus did not strive to become high-priest in the Jerusalem Temple. Rather, He waited until God appointed Him to be a high-priest in heaven after His Resurrection.

This is apparent to our author from the witness of the Scripture. For the Father not only said to Jesus, **"You *Yourself* are My Son, today I *Myself* have begotten You"** (in Ps. 2:7); He says also **in another *scripture*, "You *Yourself* are a priest forever, according to the order of Melchizedek"** (Ps. 110:4). That is, the Scripture witnesses that the Messiah is also an eternal priest.

This shows that Jesus was not high-priest because He lobbied for that role or put Himself forward for it, but because it was God's sovereign will for His Messiah. God made Jesus Messiah and enthroned Him in heaven, and God also made Him His high-priest. High-priests were always appointed by God, and that was just how Jesus was made a high-priest in heaven.

Secondly, just as high-priests lived in solidarity with those for whom they offered sacrifices, so Jesus was in solidarity with us as

III. Christ Our High Priest — Hebrews 5:5–10

one who suffered. The author of our epistle does not here refer to the primary human condition of sinfulness, but of suffering and weakness (though this is not to deny human sinfulness!). Those who offer sacrifices—and their high-priest—are portrayed primarily as weak (v. 2), not as defiantly rebellious. And Christ as our high-priest came to share our weakness as well.

This can be seen from **the days of His flesh**, the time when He walked the earth prior to His ascension to God's right hand. In the Garden of Gethsemane, for instance, **He offered up both supplications and pleas to the One able to save Him from death**. It was the Father who had all the power; Christ on earth remained at the mercy of men, just as we do. It was the Father who could **save from death**. Christ's prayers were **with** the **strong shouting** of fervency **and** with **tears**. The word translated *shouting* is the Greek *krauge*; it is used in Matt. 25:6 to describe the loud excited shouting announcing the coming of the bridegroom, and in Acts 23:9 to describe the uproarious shouting back and forth of the Pharisees and the Sadducees, which nearly resulted in a riot. Thus Christ's prayer is not portrayed as a quiet serene request, but the fervent outpouring of a soul in agony. This shows that He did indeed come to share our weakness.

The author says Christ **was heard** by God **because of His reverence** (Gr. *eulabeia*), His pious fear, the humility with which He approached His Father. This too witnesses for His complete solidarity with us in our plight. We are called to approach God with awe and reverence, and Jesus approached Him with **reverence** too. Thus, **although He was *the* Son** and shared full divinity with the Father, He still **learned obedience from what He suffered**. That is, He learned what it was to obey to the full limit of human endurance, being taught by **what He suffered**. The thought here is not that Jesus had ever disobeyed God and had to learn how to obey Him. Rather, the thought is that He learned and experienced all the hard lessons of what it meant to obey God, even though such obedience cost Him His life. He **learned** what it was to tread the path of **obedience** by never rejecting the Father's will no matter what.

It was thus that He was **made perfect** (Gr. *teleioo*; compare its use in 2:10) and reached His goal, His end (Gr. *telos*). He is now able to guide **all** His followers to glory along the same path. This is only if they **obey Him**, however, and hold fast to their Christian Faith. He abides now in heaven as **the source** (Gr. *aitios*) and fount **of eternal salvation**, the One who had been **designated by God** Himself to be our **high-priest according to the order of Melchizedek**.

The presentation of Jesus in these verses might prove a little unfamiliar to some, perhaps even jarring. We are not used to the image of Jesus offering up **supplications** and **tears** in His prayer to the Father, even though the story of His prayer in the Garden of Gethsemane should prepare us for it. Accustomed as we are to hearing about "Christ our God," we might find the complementary truth about Him being "the Man Christ Jesus" (see 1 Tim. 2:5) a bit disturbing.

Nonetheless, Orthodoxy confesses the Savior to be both perfect God and also perfect Man, consubstantial with the Father in His divinity and with us in His humanity. Part of this human consubstantiality involves His experience of prayer and of suffering. We sinners must tread the hard path of obedience in the face of pain, opposition, fear, and death, and therefore the Savior blazed the path we were to tread. To help us find the way home to salvation, it was necessary that Christ drink from the same cup from which it is our lot to drink as well. God clothed the almighty Savior in weakness (see 2 Cor. 13:4) to help us in our weakness. He immersed the Blessed One in the darkness of suffering to rescue us in our suffering. By His **strong shouting**, He brings peace to our hearts; by His **tears**, He washes the pain from the lives of men.

❧ EXCURSUS
On the Interpretation of Psalm 2:7

The text from Psalm 2:7, "You are My Son, today I have begotten You," in Christian interpretation, refers to Jesus' appointment by the Father as Messiah. In its original context, this was a hymn extolling the greatness of the House of

David. In ancient days, a king was popularly thought to be the adopted son of his god, and the day of his coronation was the day of his divine adoption. Thus even in Israel, Psalm 2 celebrates the king's adoption by God, the day when he was "begotten" by Him and became king under God's almighty protection. The nations opposing the rule of the House of David may rage as much as they want, but God Himself has begotten/adopted him as His son and will protect him accordingly.

For Christians, this psalm is fulfilled in Jesus of Nazareth, for He is the Messiah, the true descendant of David who inherits and fulfills all the glory promised to David's House. The divine begetting spoken of in Psalm 2:7 therefore also finds its fulfillment in Jesus. But what exactly does this mean?

For us who have inherited all the teaching of the Ecumenical Councils, it is difficult not to read a later terminology into these texts. We have used the title "only-begotten Son" to describe the Lord for so long that it is hard for us not to read Christ's eternal generation from the Father back into prophetic texts where it does not properly belong. Christ is indeed eternally begotten by the Father before all ages, as the Creed and the councils teach. But early interpretation of Psalm 2:7 was referring to another truth, for it reflects an earlier terminology.

In particular, it was referring to the day when Jesus of Nazareth was anointed by the Father to become the Messiah, the Anointed One, for in Jewish terminology and thought, one *becomes* the Messiah. (It is this customarily Jewish way of referring to Messiah that is reflected in Peter's speech in Acts 2:36: though eternally divine, on a certain historical day "God made Him both Lord and Christ.") This day of becoming the Anointed One, the *Meshiach* or Messiah, was the day of Jesus' Baptism, for it was then that the Father anointed Him with the Holy Spirit for His work as the Christ (Acts 10:38).

> One must, however, be clear: Jesus was always the Christ, even from the day of His birth (Luke 2:11)—He who before His earthly birth was the eternal Word of God. There is no thought here of the heresy later called "adoptionism." At His Baptism the eternal and divine Son of God, born of the Theotokos, entered upon the *office* of Messiah, and in this sense only He *became* the Christ. It was then, as Messiah, that God raised Him up and revealed Him to Israel (even as He earlier raised up David to be king; see Acts 13:22, 33).
>
> Our author here reflects this early Jewish terminology in his use of Psalm 2:7. God appointed Jesus to be Messiah at His Baptism—just as He would later make Him priest at His Ascension to His right hand.

§III.4. Press On to Maturity (5:11—6:20)

> 11 About Him we have many words *to say* and it is difficult to talk, since you have become slow of hearing.
> 12 For *though* indeed by *this* time you ought to be teachers, you again have need for someone to teach you the elements of the beginning of the oracles of God, and you have come to need milk and not solid food.
> 13 For everyone who partakes of milk is unacquainted with the word of righteousness, for he is a babe.
> 14 But solid food is for the perfect, who because of exercise have their senses trained to discern good and bad.

Mention of Christ being a "high-priest according to the order of Melchizedek" (5:10) brings our author to a spiritual impediment in his readers. Our author wanted to talk about the heavenly priesthood of Christ and how it was patterned after that of Melchizedek,

III. Christ Our High Priest — Hebrews 5:11–14

and he had **many words *to say*** about it. His hearers, however, were scarcely ready to receive such teachings as long as they remained in their spiritual infancy. As long as their whole orientation was defined by Judaism, with its earthly concerns, and as long as they were satisfied with the earthly Temple and their ancestral religion, they were in no position to appreciate the teaching he was about to give. They needed, in fact, to be jolted out of their religious complacency. They had become **slow of hearing** (Gr. *nothroi tais akoais*), spiritually lazy and sluggish. Until they repented of this and opened their minds to higher truths, it was **difficult to talk** about such heavenly matters.

It was not that they were new converts. **Indeed, by *this* time**, they **ought to be teachers** of the Faith, imparting the lessons they had learned to others. But instead of teaching others, they **again had need for someone to teach** them **the elements of the beginning of the oracles of God**. That is, they did not have a secure grip on the most basic principles taught in the Scriptures, **the oracles of God**. They needed someone to lay again their spiritual foundations.

So they had come to **need milk and not solid food**, since they were in a state of spiritual infancy and were but **babes**, unable to digest and assimilate the diet of older Christians. They were not able to absorb messages and teachings from the Scriptures about how Melchizedek was a type of Christ—indeed, they were scarcely able to absorb and internalize the basics about avoiding sexual immorality (see 12:14; 13:4). The author calls this advanced teaching **the word of righteousness** because it can be absorbed only by those who are already righteous and have reached a certain level of spiritual maturity.

By this time, ethical decisions should have become an established *habitus*, an automatic response. The Hebrew Christians should have become like those who were **perfect** and mature (Gr. *teleios*) and **who because of exercise** and constant reinforcement had their **senses trained to discern good and bad**, that is, those who had internalized and made part of themselves the rejection of evil. The words translated *exercise* (Gr. *exis*) and *trained* (Gr. *gumnazo*; compare our English word "gymnastic") have an athletic feel to them, and show that attaining spiritual maturity is a matter of discipline and exertion, such as athletes must have to attain excellence in their fields also.

> **6** 1 Therefore leaving the word of the beginning about the Christ, let us move on to perfection, not again laying a foundation of repentance from dead works and faith toward God,
> 2 of teaching about dippings, and about laying on of hands, and about the resurrection of the dead, and about eternal judgment.
> 3 And this we will do, if God allows.

Because of the fact that by this time his readers ought to be teachers (5:12), our author therefore exhorts them to **move on** quickly to **perfection** and spiritual maturity (Gr. *teleiotes*; compare the use of its cognate in 5:14). They had become stalled at the very beginning of their spiritual journey. The **word** or message consisting of **the beginning about the Christ**, the rudiments of Christian teaching, had not found a secure footing in their hearts, and their teachers needed to **again lay** such **a foundation**.

What was this rudimentary teaching, this foundation? It is described as **repentance from dead works and faith toward God**. These **dead works** were deeds that led to death. In an early church manual called the *Didache* (dating from about AD 100), such works were described as "the way of death" and consisted of such things as murder, fornication, abortion, theft, occult magic, perjury, cherishing a grudge, astrology, hypocrisy, ill temper. The list in the *Didache* was not meant to be complete or exhaustive, and such a list is not given in our present epistle at all. Our author expects his readers to be familiar from their early catechetical instruction with what was forbidden as leading to spiritual death.

We note that these **dead works** are not good works denounced as "dead" because man supposedly cannot be saved by such good works but rather by faith alone. Such a false dichotomy between good works and faith is alien to an authentic understanding of the New Testament. Rather, these **dead works** are sins, which is why one is taught here to **repent** of them. Even according to a Protestant understanding, one would not repent of good works themselves, but only of a false reliance upon them. But here the author teaches us to repent of the works themselves, showing that these works are called "dead" because they are sinful and lead to death. The author of our epistle is not teaching here the barren uselessness of good works, but rather the necessity of building life upon **repentance**.

Coupled with this as part of the spiritual foundation of faith was **faith toward God**. By this our author means the inner orientation of the believer toward his God, his inner loyalty and faithfulness to Him (the Greek word *pistis*, here translated *faith*, means both "faith" and "faithfulness"). It includes trusting God's love to save one and not relying on legalistic attempts to earn that love, as well as a zeal to do what pleases Him as disciples of Jesus the Messiah.

This foundation is also described as consisting in certain **teaching**. (In some manuscripts, the word *teaching* is in the accusative case, *didachen*, not the genitive case, *didaches*, which would suggest that the **teaching** was considered as in apposition to the **foundation**, *themelion*, which is also in the accusative case; the teaching therefore *was* the foundation.) This **teaching** consisted of instruction in certain well-established catechetical themes: **dippings**, the **laying on of hands, the resurrection from the dead,** and **eternal judgment**.

Of what did this instruction consist? It seems to have comprised the basic catechism for the Hebrew Christians, showing the main elements of the Christian worldview. The author lists them here so that his readers may once and for all accept them and internalize them—and then move on from them. Its main elements were:

1. Teaching about dippings: The word rendered *dippings* is the Greek *baptismos*. It cannot refer simply to Christian baptism, because the usual word for "baptism" is not *baptismos*, but rather *baptisma*. The word *baptismos* is elsewhere used in the New Testament to denote the dipping of cups and pitchers and copper pots as part of Jewish ritual cleansing (Mark 7:4). It is also used later in our epistle to denote the various dippings prescribed in the Law for ritual cleansing after contracting ceremonial impurity (9:10, commenting on such dippings as prescribed in Lev. 11:25; 13:6; 14:8).

Jewish proselyte baptism was based on such dippings. Building upon the notion of washing away uncleanness, the Jewish ritual prescribed for a Gentile converting to Judaism had the convert dip himself in water (after circumcision, if the convert was a male) to wash away the stain of the Gentile world. John the Forerunner's baptism was itself modeled upon such proselyte baptism, with the difference that he dared to administer such a rite to Jews.

It would appear that our author places Christian baptism (*baptisma*, "a dip") within the broader context of such pre-Christian washings (*baptismos*, "dipping"), contrasting the Christian initiation rite with its ritual forebears, teaching that the Christian rite brought with it realities not found in other washings. What were these realities? First among them is the gift of the new birth. Christ had taught that entrance into the Kingdom required a heavenly birth of water and the Spirit (John 3:3–5), and the Church has always understood this to refer to holy baptism. St. Paul referred to a "washing of rebirth" (or "regeneration," Gr. *paliggenesia*) as the means through which we are saved (Titus 3:5).

We miss the richness of this concept of rebirth, however, if we see it in strictly individualistic terms. There is a cosmic element to our regeneration. Christ referred to the age to come as the "rebirth" (Gr. *paliggenesia*) in Matthew 19:28, where it is sometimes translated as the "new world" (RSV). In the coming age, the whole cosmos will share in Christ's glory and will be reborn. Even now we Christians share in these powers of the age to come and experience this rebirth and glory. We are reborn (or "born again") in that we experience even in this age the newness of the age to come.

Baptism also bestows the remission of sins. St. Peter urged his hearers on the Day of Pentecost to "be baptized in the Name of Jesus Christ for the remission of your sins" (Acts 2:38), and Paul also was exhorted to be baptized with the words, "Arise and be baptized, and wash away your sins, calling on His Name" (Acts 22:16). In the saving bath, all our past sins are washed away, and we are initiated

III. Christ Our High Priest — Hebrews 6:1–3

into a life of repentance and forgiveness. Even infants, although having no personal sins at the time of their baptism, still receive a baptism "for the forgiveness of sins" in that baptism brings them into a relationship with Christ in which forgiveness is always available.

Finally, in baptism God grants us the gift of sonship, as we all, both men and women, become the children and heirs of God and co-heirs with Christ (Rom. 8:17). Prior to our baptism, we were children of wrath, not having access to God as our Father. But through Christ, God makes us His children (John 1:12–13), since in the font we are born of God. Thus, in baptism, we receive the adoption as sons and cry "Abba! Father!" (Gal. 4:5–6; Eph. 1:5).

These saving realities were not available through the dippings and washings of the Old Covenant. Though these availed to wash away external and ceremonial defilement (Heb. 9:10), internal and true cleansing of the heart is only available through the baptismal washing in the Church.

2. Teaching about the laying on of hands: Coming immediately after mention of *baptismos*, this **laying on of hands** almost certainly refers to the laying on of hands done in the baptismal rite of Christian initiation. As part of initiation, converts of the day were first dipped in water three times in the Name of the Father, the Son, and the Holy Spirit (Matt. 28:19) and then received the imposition of hands (possibly accompanied by anointing with oil) for the reception of the Holy Spirit (Acts 8:17; 19:6). The instruction about this rite would include telling the converts what it meant for them: the reception of the Holy Spirit and His gifts, along with God's call to use those gifts as part of the Spirit-filled Body of Christ, the Church.

The laying on of hands was also used for any act of blessing or spiritual bestowal. Thus Christ laid His hands upon the children to bless them (Mark 10:16). Thus the apostles laid hands upon candidates for ordination to bestow the Holy Spirit and church authority, making them deacons and presbyters (Acts 6:6; 14:23; 1 Tim. 4:14). Thus the presbyters laid hands on the sick to heal them (Acts 28:8; James 5:14). Christ's power was available in the Church, and it was solemnly bestowed through the laying on of hands with prayer. The teaching about the imposition of hands included teaching about the Church as the locus of divine power in the world. In the Church resided the power to heal, forgive, restore, and strengthen, for the Church was the fullness of Christ, the dwelling place of God, an island of light in a sea of darkness. These powers of healing and restoration were available to men through faith and the Name of Jesus.

3. Teaching about the resurrection of the dead: Understanding of the resurrection could not be presupposed in all Judaism of the first century, for the Sadducees did not accept it. The Pharisees did, however, as did (seemingly) the common man (compare Martha's acceptance of this teaching; John 11:24). The Christian instruction about resurrection was not limited, though, to a statement that all would one day rise again in their reconstituted bodies. It would also have revealed the central place Jesus and His rising from the dead occupied in this final resurrection of all.

Most Jews believed that when Messiah had come, the resurrection of the dead would occur, heralding and bringing the Kingdom of God. The Church taught that Jesus was the Messiah and that in His Resurrection on the third day, the final resurrection had begun. Admittedly, not all were raised at the same time as Jesus. All would come in their own order: Christ was the first-fruits, the promise of the final harvest; others would be raised (or harvested) later, at the Second Coming and the end of the age (1 Cor. 15:23). With Christ's death and Resurrection, the end of the world had begun. Jesus was the fountain and source of the final resurrection. It was not simply that all Christians would one day be raised as Jesus had been; rather, all Christians were to *share Jesus' Resurrection*. All died through their descent from and participation in Adam—and all the world would be raised through the resurrection of Christ (see 1 Cor. 15:20–24).

4. Teaching about final judgment: Once again, this instruction was not limited to a mere statement that after the final resurrection of the dead, all people would be judged. It also showed that Jesus was the

III. Christ Our High Priest — Hebrews 6:4–6

final Judge in the eternal tribunal, since He was the Messiah (John 5:22, 27). Some Jewish teaching held the view that Messiah would judge the nations (compare the Book of Enoch: "On that day My Chosen One shall sit on the throne of glory and shall try their works . . . and He shall judge the secret things and none shall be able to utter a lying word before Him"; chs. 45, 49.) The Christian Faith confirmed this Jewish expectation, teaching that Jesus of Nazareth would judge all men, since He was the Messiah (John 5:22–27). On the Last Day, all would be raised from their tombs and, in their newly constituted bodies, would stand before Christ, the universal Judge. He would speak the truth to all, rewarding the righteous for their good works and censuring the wicked for their sins. Those He confessed and accepted would share eternal life, and those He rejected would be banished to eternal Gehenna. All of our life in this age is lived in the shadow of that awe-inspiring judgment; all of our deeds are noted by the just and impartial Judge. Christian discipleship always takes thought for the final judgment.

These teachings formed the basis of the readers' catechetical instruction, and it was these basics they were in danger of forgetting. Under pressure from their Jewish countrymen, they were constantly retreating from living out their Christian worldview and needed over and over again to be retaught these fundamentals. They needed to **leave** that **word** and instruction and **move on** to greater **perfection** and maturity. The author would help them do this, **if God** would **allow** them to change their basic attitude and commit themselves to their Christian confession.

ॐ ॐ ॐ ॐ ॐ

4 For it is impossible for those who have once *for all* been enlightened and have tasted of the heavenly gift and have become partakers of the Holy Spirit,

5 and have tasted the good Word of God and the powers of the age to come,

6 and then have fallen away, to renew them again to repentance, *since* they are crucifying-again

> to themselves the Son of God and openly-disgracing Him.

The determination to move on spiritually was urgently necessary, for apostasy loomed as a real possibility for them. They must consider what they had and how much they had experienced. For they had been definitively **once *for all* enlightened**, they had **tasted of the heavenly gift** and **become partakers of the Holy Spirit**, they had **tasted the good Word of God and the powers of the age to come**. How could they throw all that away?

In these verses, we have a concise description of the reality of the Christian life and in what it consists.

First of all, it consists of being **once *for all* enlightened**. The word rendered *once for all* is the Greek *apax* (see 10:2; Jude 3). The thought here contains an idea of being definitively enlightened in the past—their illumination was not a passing phase; it was an abiding state. The word rendered *enlightened* (Gr. *photizo*) is the usual word used to describe holy baptism in the early Church. (St. Justin Martyr uses it this way in his *Apology*, ch. 61.) Our author here uses it to show how baptism brought them out of darkness and blindness into God's marvelous light (1 Pet. 2:9). Through baptism the Son of God shines His light upon us, opening our spiritual eyes to realities the world cannot see.

Their experience is also described as having **tasted the heavenly gift**. What is this **gift** (Gr. *dorea*)? Since the Holy Spirit is mentioned in the next clause, it would seem this is not a specific reference to the gift of the Holy Spirit, but to the gift of God's kindness and salvation generally. It is a **gift** in that God bestows it freely from heaven; the reference to **tasting** it probably reflects Psalm 34:8 (LXX): "Taste and see that the Lord is kind; blessed is the man who hopes in Him!" St. Peter also refers to the salvation given in baptism and speaks of experiencing God's salvation as tasting the Lord's kindness (1 Pet. 2:2–3), no doubt referring to this same psalm. Indeed, this psalm verse quickly established itself in the liturgical tradition of the Church as being a prophecy of the Eucharist, and it is likely that the reference here to **tasting** includes this eucharistic element also.

Also, they were said to have **become partakers of the Holy Spirit**. As mentioned above, the Holy Spirit was given through the laying on of hands in baptismal initiation (v. 2), and it is this experience that is referred to here. The word translated *partakers* is the Greek *metoxos*, used in 3:1 regarding the readers' partaking of their heavenly calling to sonship, and in 3:14 regarding their partaking of Christ in baptism, which will lead to their final salvation on the Last Day. Its use here is consistent with these other uses, for their partaking of the Holy Spirit was a part of their initial experience of becoming a Christian.

Finally, the readers' experience is also described as having **tasted the good Word of God and the powers of the age to come**. This is a reference to the ongoing postbaptismal experience of God's grace in the weekly Christian assembly. There they **taste** and experience **the good Word of God** in instruction, teaching, and prophecies, and through this Word they come increasingly to experience the goodness of God. There they experience **the powers of the age to come** in healings, miracles, and exorcism. Through the weekly experience of Christian worship, they access the divine power that is able to transform them, "the implanted Word, which is able to save our souls" (James 1:21), and miraculous power for their spiritual liberation (compare Gal. 3:5).

This was the experience God had given the readers of the epistle. How could they reject all of this? There was the gravest danger for them if they did reject it. If they did **fall away**, it would be **impossible to renew them again to repentance**, since they would have then joined the ranks of those who **crucify-again the Son of God and openly-disgrace Him**. That is, those Jews who did not believe in Jesus regarded Him as a deceiver. These men thought it was right to **openly-disgrace Him** on the Cross. The word translated *openly-disgrace* is the Greek *paradeigmatizo*. It is used to mean "to make a public example of someone by public punishment" (see its use in Num. 25:4 LXX). If the readers of the epistle allowed themselves to fall away, they were not simply failing to be good disciples; they were going over to join Christ's persecutors and tormentors.

What does it mean, we must ask, to say that **it is impossible to**

renew such apostates **again to repentance**? Does it mean that if one falls away, one can never return to a psychological state of contrition for the act, that one can never change one's mind, as if the act of apostasy somehow hardens one into a permanent state of rebellion whereby one *cannot* repent? This seems unlikely, for Christian history is replete with examples of people who knew the Lord, denied Him, and then went on to repent of their apostasy. (One thinks of St. Peter denying his Lord and then repenting afterward; and of St. Marcellinus, bishop of Rome [feast day June 7], who apostatized by sacrificing to the pagan gods under the persecution of Emperor Diocletian in 304, and who then repented of his apostasy and later died a martyr.) It seems then beyond dispute that lapsed Christians can repent. So what does our author mean by the phrase *renew again to repentance* (Gr. *palin anakainizein eis metanoian*)?

The clue to his meaning is found in his use of the word "repentance" in 12:17. There he writes that after Esau sold out his birthright, he "did not find a place of repentance" even though "he sought it out with tears." Certainly this lack of repentance has nothing to do with Esau's psychological state or lack of contrition. Our author cannot mean that Esau found it impossible to be sorry, for Esau was sorry to the point of tears. Rather, by saying "Esau did not find a place of repentance," our author means he found no opportunity to change his mind and to inherit the blessing of his birthright afterwards. For after Esau sold out his inheritance, there was no way he could reverse his forfeiture of the blessing.

In the same way, says our author in 12:14–17, his readers should strive for "sanctification" or they will not "see the Lord" (v. 14) and will lack the grace of God at the Last Day (v. 15). Esau irrevocably cast away his birthright, and they must not cast away their Christian Faith. If they do, on the Day of Judgment they too will find their salvation irrevocably forfeited, and then there will be no place to change their minds (v. 17).

The same meaning obtains here in 6:6. **It is impossible to renew** apostates **to repentance** in the sense that it is impossible for them to be restored to their previous blessed status *on the Last Day*. If one falls away from Christ after knowing all His blessings, any restoration to one's previous state will be impossible on the Day of Judgment. There will be no opportunity to change one's mind and to experience a renewal of the state they once knew. This presupposes, of course, that *the apostasy persists*, and that the apostates do not return to the Church during their lifetime. If they do, we are assured by the Gospel that God will always receive back the sinner who repents (1 John 1:9). The author of our epistle is not considering that situation; he is not dealing with one who believes, lapses, and then returns. The situation threatening his readers was that of believing, lapsing, and *staying lapsed*. It is in response to this situation that he warns them of the dire eternal consequences of such apostasy.

> ꙮ ꙮ ꙮ ꙮ ꙮ
>
> 7   For soil that drinks the rain which often comes upon it and brings forth plants useful to those for whom it is also farmed partakes of a blessing from God;
>
> 8   but if it brings forth thorns and thistles, *it is* unapproved and near to a curse; its end *is* for burning.

This is apparent, he writes, from a consideration of the soil. **Soil that drinks the rain which often comes upon it** and responds by **bringing forth plants useful to those for whom** the soil **is farmed**, this soil **partakes of a blessing from God**. This blessing is real. But it is no guarantee that it will always be thus. For if this same soil later **brings forth thorns and thistles**, its owners will judge it **unapproved** and worthless (Gr. *adokimos*; compare its use by Paul in 1 Cor. 9:27); this previously blessed soil will then be far from blessing. In fact, it will be **near to a curse**; whatever its past, **its end *is* for burning**. Its owners will have no choice but to set it ablaze with its thorns and thistles.

So was it with them. They had often drunk in the early and latter rains of the Spirit of God as the Spirit was poured out on all flesh (Joel 2:23, 28); they had brought forth spiritual fruit in their lives, were useful to the Lord, and partook of His blessing. But like the soil that changed, if they changed their state, they too would be judged worthless, disqualified, and fit only for God's curse. Their end too would be for burning. Let them not change their faith to faithlessness! Let them not fall away but press on to perfection.

> ॐ ॐ ॐ ॐ ॐ
> 9 But, beloved, we are persuaded of better things about you, and things that have *to do with* salvation, though indeed we are speaking thus.
> 10 For God is not unrighteous so as to forget your work and the love which you showed toward His Name, in having served the saints and in still serving them.
> 11 And we desire that each one of you demonstrate the same diligence to realize the full-assurance of hope until the end,
> 12 that you may not become slow, but become imitators of those who through faith and patience inherit the promises.

After giving such fearful warnings and speaking of being cursed and rejected by God, our author hastens to assure his readers that he is not suggesting they *are* so cursed. He addresses them as **beloved** and assures them he is **persuaded of better things** about them—indeed, **things that have *to do with* salvation**. (He uses the literary plural, calling himself **we**.)

God is not close to cursing them. **For God is not unrighteous**, as all knew; He would **not forget their work** of loving service to their brother Christians, when they **served** these **saints** (Gr. *diakoneo*) and gave them hospitality and met their needs. Indeed, they were **still serving them** and continuing their ministry of love to those in need. In this way, they were not only showing love to their fellow believers, they were **showing love toward** God's own **Name**, since they were serving their brethren for the sake of God. Thus God would not forget the love they showed Him.

Our author's **desire** was that **each one** of them would dem-

onstrate the same diligence so as to **realize the full-assurance of hope until the end**. They were doing well until now—let them not **become slow** and sluggish (Gr. *nothros*; compare its use in 5:11), let them not lose their eagerness to please God. Their zeal brought them **full-assurance**, the certainty that their **hope** of glory would be realized. Let them preserve this zeal **until the end**, that they might not forfeit their prize! If they would keep their **faith** and endure suffering with **patience**, they would **become imitators** of their illustrious forebears, the patriarchs and prophets, and like them **inherit the promises** of glory God had made to them.

🙠 🙠 🙠 🙠 🙠

13 For when God promised to Abraham, since He had no one greater to swear by, He swore by Himself,

14 saying, "Certainly blessing I will bless you and multiplying I will multiply you."

15 And thus, being patient, he attained the promise.

16 For men swear by one greater *than themselves,* and with them an oath for confirmation *is* the end of every dispute.

17 So when God intended to show even more abundantly to the heirs of the promise the unchangeableness of His intention, He mediated with an oath,

18 so that through two unchangeable things, in which *it is* impossible for God to lie, we may have strong encouragement, we who have fled-away to hold onto the hope laid-before *us,*

19 which *hope* we have as an anchor of the soul, both secure and confirmed and one which enters into the inside *behind* the curtain,

20 where Jesus has entered as a forerunner for us, having become a high-priest forever according to the order of Melchizedek.

To encourage his readers to wait with patience and perseverance, our author brings forward the great exemplar of patience, the paradigm of one who inherited the promises, their forefather Abraham. God had made promises to him, too, and had gloriously kept them.

Indeed, to encourage Abraham to persevere in his faith in Him, **when** He **promised to Abraham**, He took an oath, and **since He had no one greater to swear by, He swore by Himself**. The oath is quoted in the form given in the Greek Septuagint of Genesis 22:17. The occasion of the oath was the binding of Isaac. Abraham had shown his willingness to sacrifice even his own son Isaac to God, if God so willed; and in response to such commitment, God assured Abraham He would fulfill His promise to bless him and give him descendants through Isaac. The Hebrew original is reflected in the Septuagint version, **blessing I will bless you and multiplying I will multiply you**, with the Greek participles translating the Hebrew absolute infinitive. The grammatical effect is to intensify the verb and thus show God's determination to carry out His word.

Abraham accepted this word and, **being patient** and refusing to give up his faith in God, **attained the promise**. That is, through Isaac he was indeed blessed and multiplied, having as many descendants as there were grains of sand on the seashore (Gen. 22:17).

Our author reflects for a moment on God's use of an oath. In the case of **men**, when they swear and take an oath, they always **swear by one greater *than themselves***, usually swearing by their gods, and **with them an oath for confirmation *is* the end of every dispute**. That is, when one swears with an oath, that is taken by all as a sufficient guarantee that the one swearing will keep his word.

God wanted Abraham to have full confidence that He too would keep His word, and so when He **intended to show even more abundantly** to Abraham's **heirs** and descendants **the unchangeableness of His intention** and that He would fulfill His **promise, He mediated with an oath**. That is, He brought in between Him and those to whom He spoke an oath, swearing by Himself. (For men swear by someone greater when they bring in an oath, but there was no one greater than God, so He swore by the greatest there was—that is, by Himself.)

III. Christ Our High Priest — Hebrews 6:13–20

The point of using an oath was that God wanted to reassure Abraham, and so He used **two unchangeable things**—namely, His own word and also His oath, and since *it is* **impossible for God to lie**, Abraham need have no fear that God would not keep His promise.

And this assurance was not just meant for Abraham. The oath was given to **the heirs of the promise**—to all Abraham's descendants, which included the Jewish readers of the epistle also. The promise of God's fidelity was made to them as well, so that they too could **have strong encouragement**, they who had **fled-away** to seize and **hold onto the hope laid-before** them. God had made a promise to them as well, and through the Gospel had assured them of eternal glory if they would live as Jesus' disciples. This was their **hope,** which God had **laid-before** them as their heavenly prize. By remembering God's faithfulness to them as Abraham's heirs in the matter of His word to Abraham, they could take heart to believe God would keep this word as well.

And what a word it was! They had that hope **as an anchor of the soul**, something that could steady them when the tempests of life blew and threatened to sweep everything away. This salvation was **both secure and confirmed**, it was unshakable, it was guaranteed. They had great need of such assured hope. Everything in their world seemed to be coming loose: their Jewish non-Christian neighbors were becoming increasingly hostile, and (if we are correct in dating the epistle to AD 67) the very fabric of their life and security in Palestine was increasingly threatened. (It would soon be swept away forever by the Romans in 70.) Great waves of insecurity and suffering were washing over them, and they needed a well-anchored salvation. Their hope in Christ, who reigned supreme in heaven above all earthly tempests, offered such a salvation.

Moreover, this hope was **one which enters into the inside** of heaven itself, going ***behind*** **the curtain**. The image here (one that will be elaborated on later in the epistle) is of the earthly Tabernacle and sanctuary as a copy of the heavenly one. In the earthly sanctuary, a curtain separated the inmost shrine, the Holy of Holies, from the outer one, and that inmost shrine (originally containing the Ark) was the dwelling-place of God on earth. It becomes therefore an image of the dwelling-place of God in heaven.

Our salvation is **secure and confirmed** because **Jesus has entered as a forerunner for us** into that inmost heavenly shrine, into the very presence of God. In describing Jesus as **a forerunner**, our author reveals that we too will one day enter the very presence of God as Jesus did. Christ has opened the path, establishing free access for us as the children of God in the home of our Father. There, our author says, returning again to his first point of departure which he left in 5:10, Jesus serves as **a high-priest forever according to the order of Melchizedek**.

§III.5. Christ a High-Priest like Melchizedek (7:1–28)

Our author now begins an extended discussion of Melchizedek and his priesthood. Melchizedek was a priest-king in the time of Abraham, and he ruled over the city of Salem in southern Palestine. The full story is told in Genesis 14. As Abraham and his retainers returned from a battle, Melchizedek, as the local chieftain, went out to welcome him, bringing out bread and wine as part of a royal banquet to feast the victors. Melchizedek served as priest to his people because of his position as king, and as priest he blessed Abraham in the name of his God, *El Elyon*, "God Most High"—most likely the supreme God, the head of all the pantheon. Abraham, a devotee of Yahweh, acknowledged Melchizedek's supreme God to be the same as Yahweh and received his blessing. In return, he gave to the priest a tenth part of the choicest spoils of war he had just gathered.

It is a somewhat peculiar story in that Melchizedek is not mentioned in the Abraham stories of Genesis before he makes his sudden literary appearance in chapter 14. It is as if he appears from nowhere, blesses Abraham, and then vanishes. The reader of Genesis is not prepared for his sudden appearance, nor is he told by what right Melchizedek serves as priest. A Jewish reader of Genesis would want to see a priest's lineage before accepting the legitimacy of his priesthood; he would want to know who his father and mother were

III. Christ Our High Priest — Hebrews 7:1–3

and whether his genealogy was traceable back to the proper priestly tribe. But none of these things is said about Melchizedek. His father is not even mentioned. His origins are not stated at all, nor what became of him after he blessed Abraham.

In fact, he is not mentioned again until David mentions him in Psalm 110. There David speaks of his own descendants, saying that his royal line will have a closeness and access to God usually enjoyed only by priests—that such a one will be "a priest forever, according to the order of Melchizedek." That is, as Melchizedek was a priest and a king (for his priesthood flowed from his being king), so the Davidic king would be a priestly king too. Later Jewish interpretation would understand David to be speaking as a prophet of the messianic destiny of his line and to be describing the Messiah.

The author of the epistle focuses on Melchizedek because his life reveals the greatness of Christ. Christ, our author affirms, is our great high-priest in heaven. But how, a Jewish reader would want to know, can Jesus function as a priest—in heaven or anywhere else? For Jesus was of the tribe of Judah, not Levi, and Moses in the Law said that only those from the tribe of Levi could be priests.

The answer is this prophecy of David's in Psalm 110:4, where the messianic descendant of David is said to be a priest "according to the order of Melchizedek." That is, Jesus is a high-priest *by virtue of His being King*, just as Melchizedek was. It is because He is the Messiah and King that He is also Priest.

Moreover, He is a better priest than any of the Jewish levitical priests, for His priesthood is of a higher order. The priesthood of Melchizedek, our author argues, is superior to the priesthood that would later be established for Levi under Moses in the Law. Therefore, Jesus' priesthood is superior to the priesthood functioning in Jerusalem. How then could the readers cast away such a superior priesthood for an inferior one?

---

7 1 For this Melchizedek, king of Salem, priest of the Most High God, who met Abraham as he

> was returning from the slaughter of the kings and blessed him,
> 2 to whom also Abraham divided up a tithe of everything, was first of all, which *is* being translated, king of righteousness, and then also king of Salem, which is king of peace.
> 3 Without father, without mother, without genealogy, having neither beginning of days nor end of life, but resembling the Son of God, he remains a priest forever.

Our author begins to build his case. Melchizedek is a type or foreshadowing of Messiah, and our author begins to unpack the typology of the account in Genesis 14. **Melchizedek** is there described as **king of Salem**, a town in southern Palestine probably to be identified with Jerusalem. **Salem**, of course, suggests a connection with the Hebrew *shalom*, or "peace," and so our author is able to describe him as the **king of peace**. Also, the very name **Melchizedek** makes the same point, for when it is **translated** literally it means **king of righteousness** (originally, perhaps, "our king is righteous," the "king" in his name being a reference to God). By describing Melchizedek as both **king of peace** and **king of righteousness**, our author is able to show that Melchizedek is a true type of Christ. Christ is the only One truly described as King of Peace and King of Righteousness. All other kings are stained with the blood of war and are fallen sinners. The Messiah alone can be designated with such exalted titles, and by showing that Melchizedek is so described, our author establishes him as a true type of the Messiah.

Melchizedek's typological qualifications are confirmed by other ways he is described—or rather by ways he is *not* described. What is amazing about a description of a priest in a Jewish book is the absence of any **father, mother,** or **genealogy**, for by Jewish reckoning it is just these things that establish a person's priesthood.

Also, his **beginning of days** (that is, where he came from) is not mentioned, nor his **end of life** (that is, what became of him). It is as if he comes from nowhere and then vanishes. His end is not narrated; literarily speaking, **he remains a priest forever**. That is, in the literary narrative, he remains a numinous figure, **resembling the Son of God**; his almost supernatural appearance in Genesis makes him an appropriate type of the supernatural Messiah.

Because of the confusion occasioned by these verses in the history of the Church, it may be added that our author is not saying that Melchizedek never died or that he actually remains alive continuously. The writer of our epistle is speaking of the *literary portrayal* of Melchizedek in Scripture, not of the historical figure himself. The historical figure doubtless did die, as do all men. It is the literary narrative and its typological significance that alone concern our author.

> ꙮ ꙮ ꙮ ꙮ ꙮ
>
> 4 Now observe how great this one *was* to whom Abraham the patriarch gave a tithe of the spoils.
> 5 And those indeed of the sons of Levi who receive the priestly-office have a commandment in the Law to collect *a tithe* from the people, that is from their brothers, although they *also* have come out from the loins of Abraham.
> 6 But the one whose genealogy is not from them collected *a tithe* from Abraham and blessed the one who had the promises.
> 7 But without any contradiction the lesser is blessed by the greater.
> 8 And here dying men receive tithes, but there one of whom it is witnessed that he lives.
> 9 And, so to say, through Abraham even Levi, who received tithes, paid *tithes*,
> 10 for he was still in the loins of his father when Melchizedek met him.

Having established that Melchizedek is a type or foreshadowing of Messiah, our author bids his readers **observe how great** was **this one**, Melchizedek, **to whom Abraham gave a tithe of the spoils** of his battle. For having established that Christ is a priest "after the order of Melchizedek," it is also necessary to establish that this Melchizedek kind of priesthood is superior to the Aaronic kind of priesthood. It would not do to say that Christ had a priesthood inferior to the priesthood of the Temple, as if His priesthood were a kind of consolation prize for those Christians denied access to the synagogue or Temple. Rather, our author has to demonstrate that the Melchizedek priesthood of Christ is superior to the priesthood of the Temple, so that even if Christians were deprived of the Temple sacrifices, they still had a better priesthood and sacrifice through their faith in Christ.

Our author makes his argument for the superiority of Christ's priesthood by demonstrating the superiority of Melchizedek over Aaron. He begins to do this by showing the superiority of Melchizedek over Abraham, pointing out that Melchizedek **collected a tithe from Abraham and blessed** him, that is, blessed the very one **who had the promises** of God. This shows that Melchizedek was greater than Abraham, for in giving Melchizedek a tithe of the spoils and receiving his blessing in return, Abraham acknowledged that Melchizedek was greater than he. Giving the priest the tithe showed this, since the tithe was meant as a kind of tribute. Further, receiving the priest's blessing showed this as well, for **without any** fear of **contradiction**, all could affirm that **the lesser is blessed by the greater**.

Thus not only was Melchizedek greater than Abraham, he was greater than Abraham's descendant **Levi** too (the founder of the levitical priesthood working at the Jerusalem Temple). Some may have suggested that though Levi was a descendant of Abraham, he was nonetheless greater than Abraham and therefore also greater than Melchizedek. Not so, says our author. In blessing Abraham, Melchizedek showed his superiority over Levi as well, since Levi was **still in the loins of his father** Abraham **when Melchizedek met him**. Thus, **so to say, through Abraham even Levi, who received tithes** from his fellow Israelites under the Law, **paid *tithes*** to Melchizedek, thereby acknowledging the priest-king's superiority.

This last argument sounds strange to modern ears, since we are accustomed by our secular culture to think of personhood only in

III. Christ Our High Priest — Hebrews 7:11–14

individualistic terms. But that is a mistake and should not blind us to the biblical fact that as persons we are also defined by our larger history. According to this insight, persons are all derivative, both spiritually as well as biologically, and one's significance *within one's social group* is determined by one's origins. This does not mean that God cannot call one to a place beyond the restrictive confines of one's social group. But it does mean that within the biblical world of the ancient Middle East, one's tribal origins were fundamental to who one was and to one's function in society. Our author's argument here is not forced but must be seen within its cultural context.

> 11 If therefore perfection was through the levitical priesthood (for on the basis of it the people received-the-Law), what *was the* further need for another priest to arise according to the order of Melchizedek and not be named according to the order of Aaron?
> 12 For when the priesthood is changed, of necessity a change of the Law happens also.
> 13 For the one of whom these things are spoken belongs to another tribe, from which no one has attended to the altar.
> 14 For it is *quite* plain that our Lord sprang from Judah, a tribe concerning which Moses spoke nothing about priests.

Our author now begins to draw his conclusions. The Scripture (in Psalm 110:4) had shown that Messiah was to be a priest according to the order of this above-mentioned Melchizedek. Did this not prove the insufficiency for the Kingdom of God of the levitical priesthood then functioning in Jerusalem? For **if perfection** (that is, accomplishing all that God intended for His people in the messianic age) **was through the levitical priesthood**, then **what** *was the* **further need for another priest**—that is, Messiah—**to arise**

87

according to the order of Melchizedek and not be named according to the order of Aaron? That is, why was Messiah's priesthood to be different from the normal Jewish priesthood?

For it is *quite* plain (Gr. *prodelon*) that **our Lord sprang from the tribe of Judah, a tribe concerning which Moses in the Law spoke nothing about priests.** According to the way God had arranged things in the Law of Moses, no one from the tribe of Judah was allowed to **attend to the altar**; that was only for those from the tribe of Levi. Jesus was descended from the tribe of Judah, but this was according to the providence of God. He did not *need* to come from Judah—God could have arranged it so that He sprang from the tribe of Levi if He had so willed, and then Jesus could have functioned as a levitical priest. The question is: Why did God so arrange it that Messiah's priesthood would be of a different kind from that of the Levites and the house of Aaron?

The answer is that the levitical priesthood and the Law generally could not perfect anyone (vv. 11, 19). The priesthood and the Law were intertwined, so that **when the priesthood is changed, of necessity a change in the Law happens also**. The Law with its levitical and earthly priesthood was sufficient to accomplish what God intended for it during its time. But it could not bring the sinner to a state of cleansing and inner transformation. It was insufficient for the realities of the Kingdom of God. And therefore the Messiah, the One who inaugurates the Kingdom of God, must be of a different order and have a different kind of priesthood.

One must not miss how radical it was for a Jew like our author to assert that **a change in the Law happens also**. Jews considered the Law to be eternal, unchangeable, God's last word to Israel and the world. It was almost unthinkable to assert that this Law must change or could be replaced (compare 8:13). But that is what our author here asserts. For him, that the Messiah would have a priesthood other than that of Levi meant that the entire superstructure of the Law was being transcended and replaced, for this priesthood was at the heart of the Law. This little verse about the messianic priesthood of Melchizedek had a tremendous and far-reaching significance.

III. Christ Our High Priest   Hebrews 7:15–19

> ✿ ✿ ✿ ✿ ✿
>
> 15 And this is more abundantly *thoroughly* plain, if another priest arises according to the likeness of Melchizedek,
> 16 who has become *a priest* not according to the Law of fleshly commandment, but according to the power of an indestructible life.
> 17 For it is witnessed *of Him*, "You *Yourself* are a priest forever according to the order of Melchizedek."
> 18 For there is, on the one hand, a nullifying of a former commandment because of its weakness and uselessness
> 19 (for the Law perfected nothing), and on the other hand the introduction of a better hope, through which we draw near to God.

Our writer moves further to argue his case and to compare Christ with the levitical high-priests throughout the centuries. When he does this, his case is more clear and compelling. It is not just "plain" (Gr. *delon*) or even "quite plain" (Gr. *prodelon*; compare v. 14), but **abundantly *thoroughly* plain** (Gr. *perissoteron katadelon*). Anyone comparing Christ with the Jerusalem priests could see that the time for the older priesthood was drawing to its end.

For consider the following: First of all, the Aaronic priesthood was served by "dying men" (v. 8), by priests who were mortal and "many in number," succeeding one after another because each one in turn was "forbidden by his death from remaining on" as priest (v. 23). Christ, however, was not appointed to His office **according to the Law of** mere **fleshly commandment** (that is, of a Law dealing with things of the flesh and of merely outward effects). He became a priest **according to the power of an indestructible life**, a life no longer limited by this world of flesh. Thus, in the likeness of Melchizedek (whose "end of life" was not mentioned in Scripture; v. 3), Christ lives on forever (v. 8).

The significance of this is prophesied in the Scriptures, for in Psalm 110:4 **it is witnessed *of Him*, "You *Yourself* are a priest forever according to the order of Melchizedek."** In its original context, this **forever** doubtless meant simply "permanently" and that God would not remove His priesthood from the king. But as a prophecy of Christ, this word **forever** witnesses to His **indestructible life** and the fact that He holds His high-priesthood in heaven, far above this earthly realm of death, where He sits triumphantly in the power of His Resurrection.

This comparison shows clearly that God was in the process of **nullifying** and setting aside the **former commandment because of its weakness and uselessness. The Law perfected nothing**; it could not transform the sinful and mortal nature of men, and so it had no lasting place in the messianic Kingdom of God. With Jesus' Cross and Ascension, one had **the introduction** and bringing forward **of a better hope**, one **through which we** could now **draw near to God** and be transformed.

༄ ༄ ༄ ༄ ༄

20 And inasmuch as *it was* not without an oath-taking

21 (for they indeed became priests without an oath-taking, but He with an oath-taking, through the One who said to Him, "The Lord has sworn and will not change *His mind*, 'You *Yourself* are a priest forever'"),

22 according to such *an oath* Jesus also has become the guarantee of a better covenant.

23 And on the one hand, the *former* priests were many in number, because they were forbidden by death from remaining on,

24 but on the other hand, because He remains forever, He has a permanent priesthood.

25 Hence also He is able to save completely those who come *near* to God through Him, since He always lives to appeal for them.

III. Christ Our High Priest Hebrews 7:20–25

Our author makes a second comparison of Christ with the levitical high-priests to show His superiority to them. When Christ's priesthood was inaugurated by God, it was **not without an oath-taking**. The levitical high-priests **indeed** entered their office **without such an oath-taking**. God appointed Aaron and his descendants to serve at His earthly altar (Ex. 28:1), but He uttered no oath regarding permanency. But it was otherwise with Christ's priesthood, and the presence of God's oath testifies to the superiority of His priesthood.

This is seen in the Scripture mentioned earlier. For Psalm 110:4 reads, "**The Lord** [that is, God] **has sworn and will not change *His mind*, 'You are a priest forever'.**" By not only appointing the Son of David **a priest forever**, but by also declaring that He **had sworn** this and given His oath, one about which He **will not change *His mind*** God shows His zeal in establishing His priesthood with a permanency the Aaronic priesthood lacked.

Thus **Jesus also has become the guarantee of a better covenant**. He will **remain on forever**, having **a permanent priesthood**. Death can never touch Him, since He has **arisen** and come before God in "indestructible life" (vv. 15–16).

Because of this, **He is able to save completely** (Gr. *eis to panteles*; "entirely," "to the uttermost," "to all ages") **those who come *near* to God through Him**. If His disciple joins in the worship of the Church, and if in the Church's prayer he draws near to the throne of grace (4:16), he comes to the heavenly Jerusalem and finds that Jesus' Blood speaks better than the blood of Abel (12:22, 24). Through the heavenly intercession of Jesus, the great high-priest, one can come to God boldly and with confidence.

This is because Jesus **always lives to appeal for** them. This appeal and intercession should not be thought of in carnal, mechanistic terms, as if the glorified Christ is forever engaged in a string of verbal prayers and legal appeals to the Father. Rather, He appeals for His Church and intercedes for them because *He is Himself that intercession*. He is the Lamb slain (Rev. 5:6), and His presence at the right hand of God *is itself the appeal to the Father*.

The actual nature of Christ's glorified state, and how it surpasses the limits of time and space, is not revealed to us. We cannot know how He can be present to all His many children as each one prays and offers supplications, though we may be sure that He is so present and hears each prayer. The author of our epistle, however, is not here speaking of that. He is speaking of how we His Church, as sinners, may draw near to the holy God. Our freedom of access, he says, is by Christ's presence with the Father and by His sprinkled Blood (12:24).

> ༓ ༓ ༓ ༓ ༓
> 26 For it was proper that we should have such a high-priest, holy, guileless, undefiled, having been separated from sinners and having become higher than the heavens;
> 27 who does not have necessity daily, like those high-priests, to offer sacrifices, first for his own sins *and* then for those of the people, for this One did *this* once *for all* when He offered Himself.
> 28 For the Law appoints men *as* high-priests who have weakness, but the word of the oath-taking, *which came* after the Law, *appoints* a Son, made perfect forever.

That we have such a high-priest is **proper** and fitting. That is, the transcendent nature of the Kingdom of God demands that **we should have such** a transcendent **high-priest**. For in the Kingdom of God death is abolished, and we are perfected, healed of our sins, and transformed so as to become immortal. Therefore, the high-priest who is the covenant guarantee and minister of such a salvation must Himself be beyond the reach of sin and death.

Christ sits therefore at the right hand of the Father, **holy** and devout (Gr. *osios*; compare its use in Titus 1:8), **guileless** and uncorrupted (Gr. *akakos*), **undefiled** and uncontaminated (Gr. *amiantos*). Unlike the high-priests his readers have known (such as Annas and Caiaphas), Christ has been **separated from sinners** and has no part in their counsels. He has **become higher than the heavens** and is far above the intrigue, corruption, and moral weakness that have long plagued earthly high-priests.

Those high-priests are sinners, and each one has **necessity daily to offer sacrifices, first for his own sins and then for those of the people**. Even the best and most devout of them (one thinks of the famously righteous high-priest Simon the son of Onias, celebrated in Sirach 50:1–21) still had **weakness**.

But Christ is superior to them. He does **not have necessity** to continue day after day to labor at the altar, standing there **to offer sacrifices**. This priestly work He **did once *for all* when He offered Himself** on the Cross. **The Law appoints men *as* high-priests who** are weak and who still labor under the constraints of sin and mortality. **The word** of God, given in prophetic **oath-taking** that witnesses to His eternity (Ps. 110:4), ***appoints* a Son made perfect forever**, placed beyond the power of death.

§III.6. Christ's Priesthood Greater than Aaron's (8:1—10:18)

ॐ ॐ ॐ ॐ ॐ

8 1 Now the sum of what has been said is this: We have such a high-priest, who has sat down at the right *hand* of the throne of the Greatness in the heavens,
2 an offerer in the *Holy* of Holies and the true tent, which the Lord set up, not man.

After an extended comparison of Melchizedek with the levitical priesthood, our author brings his argument to a head, saying **the sum** (Gr. *kephalaion*, "the head or chief point") **of what has been said is this: We have such a high priest**. Jesus has **sat down at the right *hand* of the throne of the Greatness in the heavens**, sharing all the authority of the Father. (We note the characteristically Jewish circumlocution, referring to God as **the Greatness in the heavens**.) Jesus is present before God as an **offerer in the *Holy* of**

Holies, one who serves in **the true tent**, the heavenly Tabernacle **which the Lord** God **set up, not man**. The word rendered *offerer* is the Greek *leitourgos*; its cognates, such as the noun *leitourgia*, are used in the Greek Septuagint to describe the cultic and ritual services of the priests in the Temple (compare Ex. 28:35 LXX, which speaks of Aaron "serving" [*leitourgein*] in his sacred vestments). Christ is an **offerer** of holy things before God in that He serves as a priest before Him. And since Christ's is a heavenly priesthood, it is indisputably and immeasurably superior to the priesthood of the levitical priests on earth.

> ༺ ༺ ༺ ༺ ༺
>
> 3 For every high-priest is appointed to offer up both gifts and sacrifices; hence it is necessary that this one also have something to offer up.
> 4 If therefore He were on earth, He would not be a priest, since there are those who offer up the gifts according to the Law;
> 5 who *offer* worship in a model and shadow of the heavenly things, just as Moses was warned when he was about to complete the Tent, for, "See," He says, "that you make all things according to the pattern which was shown to you on the mountain."

As a priest, He must **have something to offer up,** since that is what **every high-priest is appointed** to do. What is the nature of this offering and of this service?

It cannot be simply a heavenly version of what the levitical priests do, offering the sacrifices of dead animals. Christ is not a heavenly Levite. Indeed, **if He were on earth, He would not be a priest** at all, **since there are those who offer up** those kind of animal sacrifices **according to the Law**. God has plenty of Levites already to offer up the blood of animals. He does not need Christ to be a priest like that.

Christ's priesthood and service is of an utterly transcendent kind, and it differs from the service of the Levites as heaven differs from earth. The Levites who serve in the earthly Tabernacle and Temple *offer* **worship** (Gr. *latreuo*, "to serve and offer cultic service"; compare its use in Acts 7:7) in a mere **model** and copy of the true Tabernacle, a mere **shadow** of the heavenly reality.

This is apparent from God's original instruction to **Moses**, when He **warned** him when Moses **was about to complete** the building of **the Tent**. At that time, in the wilderness of Mount Sinai, God gave Moses detailed instructions for building the Tabernacle, giving him a vision of His heavenly glory **on the mountain**. And when the time came for Moses to actually construct the sacred site, God referred to this vision as a **pattern** (Gr. *tupos;* Ex. 25:40 LXX). That is, the earthly Tent was to be a type and representation of the heavenly one; the earthly dwelling place of God, a symbol of His heavenly dwelling. The Levites on earth therefore served in this copy and shadow; Christ serves in the reality itself.

℘ EXCURSUS
On the Tabernacle and Temple as Antitypes

The ancients, influenced by Platonic concepts, spoke of type and antitype (Gr. *tupos* and *antitupos*, translated here as "pattern" and "corresponding pattern"). In Platonic thought, there exists a realm of transcendent realities, "ideas" (the types), of which earthly realities are the pale copy (the antitypes). In the days of the apostles, even those who were not thorough-going Platonists still used this kind of vocabulary, since it expressed a universal truth. As early as the Babylonians, people considered, for example, that the earthly temples of the gods reflected and imaged the heavenly dwellings of the gods, and the words for "house" and "temple" referred both to the earthly temple of the god and to his heavenly abode. This usage is reflected in the Old Testament as well: in Psalm 18:6, David speaks of God hearing from "His Temple," meaning His heavenly abode, since the earthly Temple of Solomon had not yet been built.

Given this background, it is natural that Jews around the time of Christ should think the Tabernacle built by Moses reflected God's heavenly dwelling. Philo (an Alexandrian Jew much influenced by Platonism who was an older contemporary of Jesus) wrote that Moses "saw with the soul's eye the immaterial ideas of the material objects [of the Tabernacle] which were about to be made" (*Life of Moses*, ch. 2). That is, on Mount Sinai, Moses saw the heavenly "idea" of the Tabernacle and its furnishings, the heavenly dwelling-place of God, the *tupos*, and it was on the basis of this vision that he built the Tabernacle, the *antitupos*.

This understanding is reflected in Wisdom 9:8 as well. There the author writes, "You [God] have given a command to build a Temple on Your holy mountain, and an altar in the city of Your habitation, a copy of the holy Tabernacle that You prepared from the beginning." The understanding is the same as in Philo: God prepared "a holy Tabernacle," a heavenly dwelling-place for Himself "from the beginning," and the Temple with its altar on earth is but "a copy" of it.

The author of our epistle uses this same vocabulary. Without subscribing to all the tenets of Platonism, he acknowledges that Moses saw God in His heavenly glory, and that the earthly Tabernacle was meant to reflect this glory. The heavenly abode of God was the *tupos*; the earthly Tabernacle was the *antitupos,* the antitype. Given this, it follows naturally that all the earthly ministries performed in the earthly antitype are but pale reflections of heavenly realities—and foreshadowings of Christ's heavenly ministry. The Levites offering sacrifices in the Temple, for all their glittering pomp, are mere antitypes. Christ, reigning as high-priest in heaven, is the true Offerer, the *tupos*, the abiding reality.

III. Christ Our High Priest — Hebrews 8:6–12

> ❧ ❧ ❧ ❧ ❧
>
> 6 But now He has attained a more outstanding offering-*ministry*, by as much as He is also the mediator of a better covenant, which has been enacted on better promises.
> 7 For if that first *one* had been blameless, there would have been no place sought for a second.

Thus, Christ **has attained a more outstanding offering-*ministry*** (Gr. *leitourgia*), a more excellent priesthood. This reflects the superiority of the **covenant** of which He is the priestly **mediator**. This covenant is **better** because it **has been enacted on better promises**. That is, the covenant Christ's priesthood serves leads to God in a way the Jewish covenant never could. The superiority of Christ's covenant over the Jewish one is shown in the very fact that this second covenant exists. **For if that first** Jewish covenant **had been blameless** and had been able to accomplish all God willed to accomplish for men in the Kingdom of God, **there would have been no place sought for a second** covenant. The fact that God bypassed the levitical arrangements in glorifying Christ as a high-priest before Him shows the inadequacy of the levitical priesthood.

> ❧ ❧ ❧ ❧ ❧
>
> 8 For blaming them, He says, "Behold, days are coming, says the Lord, when I will consummate a new covenant with the house of Israel and with the house of Judah;
> 9 "not like the covenant which I made with their fathers on the day when I took them by the hand to lead them out from the land of Egypt; for they did not remain in My covenant, and I *Myself* neglected them, says the Lord.
> 10 "For this *is* the covenant that I will decree for the house of Israel after those days, says the Lord; I will put My laws into their mind and I

> will write them upon their hearts and will be God to them and they themselves will be My people.
> 11 "And they will not teach each one his *fellow* citizen and each one his brother, saying, 'Know the Lord!' for all will know Me, from the littlest to the greatest of them.
> 12 "For I will be merciful to their unrighteous *acts* and I will *certainly* not remember their sins any longer."

This statement that the Mosaic Covenant was inadequate is an audacious one for a Jew to make. The permanency and glory of the Mosaic Covenant were axiomatic for a Jew. What was this talk of it being blamed as inadequate?

Our author makes his point in the typically Jewish way by an extensive quote from the Scripture, citing Jeremiah 31:31–34. The fact that the Jewish Covenant was not blameless and that God was **blaming them** as inadequate is shown by the fact that for the Kingdom, God would **consummate a new covenant**. If the first covenant was sufficient to serve as a vehicle for the Kingdom, why bring in a new one?

And more than that, the **new covenant** God would **decree for the house of Israel** would be **not like the** older **covenant** He **made on the day when** He lovingly **took them by the hand to lead them out from the land of Egypt** under Moses. That Mosaic covenant would prove its limitations through Israel's continued apostasy. There were countless times when Israel **did not remain in** God's **covenant**, and God in turn **neglected them**, turning His back on them and selling them into the hands of their enemies (see Judg. 2:11–21). For the Mosaic covenant could do no more than reveal the truth and the way of righteousness. The history of Israel proved abundantly that the covenant could not empower Israel to keep it. The first covenant remained an external one, written only on tablets of stone (2 Cor. 3:3).

It would be otherwise with the new covenant. This covenant

would be **written upon their hearts**. It would involve the internal transformation and healing of human nature, as God would **put His laws into** the people's **mind**. There would be no more need for prophets and the faithful remnant to rebuke the people for apostasy, exhorting them to repent of their idolatry and saying, **"Know the Lord!" for all** in Israel would **know** Him, **from the littlest** and humblest worshipper **to the greatest** sage and king.

Thus the ancient promises of intimate communion with God would at last be fulfilled, and He **would be God** to His covenant people, blessing and protecting them, and **they themselves would be** His faithful **people**. Such would be the extent of the people's transformation that God would **be merciful to their unrighteous acts** and *certainly* **not remember their sins any longer**. (The Greek negative is quite emphatic—not a simple negative *ou*, but the more intensive *ou me*.)

To "remember" in the Scriptures is not simply to recall something mentally; it is to take action. Thus God would "remember" Israel when they went into battle by granting them victory (Num. 10:9); thus the widow of Zarephath thought God had remembered her iniquity when a catastrophe struck her house (1 Kin. 17:18). God "remembers" Israel's sins when He brings judgment upon them for their apostasy.

It was this judgment that was to be a thing of the past. The Israel of the new covenant would be so transformed through the sacrificial work of Christ that judgment (such as was experienced in the Babylonian Exile) would be experienced no more. Thus the covenant over which Christ served as high-priest was indeed better than the older one served by the Levites (v. 6), for the new one contained promises of this inner cleansing and transformation.

ॐ ॐ ॐ ॐ ॐ

13 When He said, "a new *covenant*," He has made the first obsolete. But whatever is being made obsolete and is *growing* old *is* near to disappearing.

Our author has a final point to make in his explication of the prophecy of the new covenant in Jeremiah 31. Not only did mention of **a new *covenant*** mean that the first one was insufficient and unable to effect inner cleansing; it also meant that **the first** was being **made obsolete**. The Greek word translated here *make obsolete* is *palaioo*. It is the word used in 1:11 for the eventual wearing out of the cosmos, and it is related to the word *palaios*, "old."

And this in turn meant the Jewish covenant, since it was ***growing old***, was **near to disappearing** and to being abolished. The thought is of the Jewish covenant growing so old that it finally expires, and of having lived out all its days so that it is ready to die of old age. (The word translated *growing old* is the Gr. *gerasko*, from which the English word "geriatric" is derived.) All this being so, how could the readers of the epistle fall away from Christ the heavenly high-priest for the sake of Judaism, which was even then being replaced?

❧ EXCURSUS
On the Abolition of the Old Covenant

When the author of Hebrews speaks of the Old Covenant as having been "made obsolete" and "near to disappearing," he is speaking of the Law of Moses and the whole ancestral inheritance of Judaism. His sole point is that the Law functioned to preserve Israel as a distinct people, to teach Israel certain lessons and so prepare them for the coming of Christ. Now that Christ had come, the Law, *as a covenantal way of life*, was obsolete. All its provisions (such as circumcision, the dietary laws, the offering of sacrifices) were no longer necessary. They were only ever intended by God to remain in force "until a time of improvement" or reforms (9:10), when Christ came as the true and eternal high-priest.

Now that Christ presides in heaven for us, we no longer need these provisions. They may have cultural significance and value, but they are no longer the indispensable requirement for God's covenant people. Jews may still circumcise their children and refrain from eating pork, since these are marks of their cultural and national inheritance. But such things are no longer the *sine qua non* of being God's people. In Christ, neither circumcision nor uncircumcision matters—only a new creation (Gal. 6:15).

None of this implies that Israel, as a nation, has no more place in God's purposes. The Jewish people remain God's people, even if their status is now somewhat ambiguous. God's calling remains irrevocable (see Rom. 11:29), so that the Jews still retain a special status before God. But that status is in itself no guarantee of blessing, for divine blessing only comes through obedience, and in knowingly rejecting Jesus, the Jewish people have consigned themselves to enmity in God's sight. Thus, from the standpoint of their status as God's people, they are beloved for the sake of the patriarchs, and they remain God's people. But from the standpoint of divine blessing, they are the enemies of God because they reject the Gospel (Rom. 11:28). That is, the Gospel and the Kingdom belong to them by right, but they will not profit from this unless they repent and have faith in Jesus their Messiah. As long as they steadfastly and knowingly reject Jesus, they remain (like the rest of the unbelieving and rejecting world) objects of divine wrath. As Jews, they are "sons of the Kingdom." But, like any unbeliever, even the sons of the Kingdom will be cast out into the outer darkness if they persist in rebellion against God's will (see Matt. 8:12).

This is no different from their status in the days of the old covenant prior to the coming of Christ. During the idolatrous days of the sixth century BC, the Jewish people (then the tribe of Judah) remained God's covenant people. Nonetheless, because of their disobedience and idolatry, God rejected them, disowned them, and treated them as His enemies, sending upon them judgment and exile in Babylon. In the same way, the Jewish people remain today

> God's people. But this will bring only judgment unless they receive baptism as the disciples of the Messiah Jesus. Blessing and salvation only come through faith in Him.

> ❧ ❧ ❧ ❧ ❧
>
> **9** 1 Therefore even the first *covenant* had requirements of worship and the worldly Holy *Place*.
> 2 For there was a Tent built, the first *one*, in which were the lampstand and the table and the breads of presentation; this is called the Holy *Place*.
> 3 And behind the second curtain, *there was* a Tent which is called the Holy of Holies,
> 4 having a golden incense-altar and the ark of the covenant covered on all sides with gold, in which was a golden jar having the manna, and the rod of Aaron which sprouted, and the tables of the covenant.
> 5 Above it were the cherubim of glory overshadowing the mercy seat; about which things it is not possible now to speak in detail.

Our author had already intimated in 8:3–4 that Christ's priesthood was utterly unlike the levitical one in the earthly Temple of Jerusalem, and he now begins to describe it further. To do this, he contrasts it with the priesthood operating in **the first *covenant*** that God established through Moses.

In describing the physical arrangements of the Mosaic covenant, our author focuses on those of the first Tent (the portable one used from the time of Moses to David), rather than the more imposing permanent structure built by Solomon or even the later structure rebuilt after the Exile, which was currently in use. This was because this first Tent was simpler than the other two (being constructed in

III. Christ Our High Priest   Hebrews 9:1–5

such a way that it could be disassembled, moved, and reassembled) and thus more suited to revealing its merely temporary and provisional character.

Thus the Mosaic covenant had **requirements of worship** (that is, things which were needed for the performance of the cult) and also a **worldly Holy *Place*** (Gr. *agion kosmikon*), or an earthly sanctuary, one having the characteristics and limitations of life in this world (Gr. *kosmos*). The actual arrangements are described in depth in Exodus 25–30 and summarized here. This earthly sanctuary consisted of a **Tent built** or erected, the **first** or outer one. In this Tent were the seven-branched **lampstand** (the so-called *menorah*) and a **table** on which were placed the twelve **breads of presentation** (sometimes called the showbread), which were symbolic of the life of the twelve tribes of Israel. This outer Tent was **called the Holy *Place*.**

Inside the Holy Place **behind** a **second curtain** was a second Tent, **called the Holy of Holies**, which was the inmost shrine, the earthly dwelling-place for the God of Israel. Attached to this shrine was **a golden incense-altar,** which stood before it in the Holy Place. In a pagan temple, this inmost shrine would be occupied by a statue or image of the deity, but the God of Israel strictly forbade such images, and so this inner shrine was empty of such idols. Their place was taken by **the ark of the covenant**, which was **covered on all sides with gold.**

Inside this ark or sacred chest had been placed a **golden jar having the manna** with which Israel had been fed during the days of wandering in the wilderness; **the rod of Aaron which sprouted**, by which his priesthood was vindicated against challengers; and finally, the small stone **tables of the covenant** which Moses received from God on Mount Sinai (Ex. 16:32–34; 25:16; Num. 17:10). **Above** this ark were **the cherubim of glory**, the golden images of angels affixed to the top of the ark and **overshadowing the mercy seat** of gold, the place where atonement was made. God in heaven was attended by the true cherubim; here on earth there could only be their reflection in the carved images. Each of these things had its own special significance, but it was **not possible** for the author **to speak in detail** about them, lest his epistle be too long.

Why mention such arrangements? Our author wants to stress the earthly nature of the levitical covenant and how it involves merely physical things such as objects of furniture. The Mosaic Tent contained such things as would be found in anyone's house—a table, bread, a jar, a lampstand. Moreover, the ark contained souvenirs of Israel's historical wandering (a jar for the manna Israel ate, Aaron's rod that sprouted, the tablets Moses received), and these witnessed to the earthbound nature of the covenant.

True, the Mosaic priesthood had a glory, but it was a merely earthly glory, consisting of **gold** (this gold is mentioned three times, as covering the incense-altar, the ark, and the jar). The glory of the new covenant, by contrast, consisted of the glory of God Himself. Thus, all the physical arrangements for the first covenant revealed it as belonging entirely to this world and this age.

❧ EXCURSUS
On the Significance of the Temple Furnishings

Since the author of our epistle declines to "speak in detail" about the significance of the Temple furnishings, any explanation of its typological meaning can only be offered tentatively. But I would suggest the following.

In the outer Tent, the Holy Place, God ordered Israel to place a *lampstand* with seven lights. This burned before the God of Israel and was an image of His abiding Presence in the midst of His people. As the lights never went out, so God would never abandon His people. I would suggest this is a type and prophecy of Christ, the Light of the world. As the lampstand supported the fire, so Mary the Theotokos gave birth to Christ. Christ is the burning Light, she the lampstand.

The outer Tent also contained *a table* and the *breads of presentation*, often called the showbread. These were twelve loaves of bread, renewed every Sabbath and eaten by the priests. From their number, it is plain that they represent the twelve tribes of Israel. They also are a type of Christ, the Bread of Heaven, who is Himself the embodiment of Israel. This indicates an identity of the Lord and His people, for the bread images both Israel and Christ. This is fulfilled in the Church, for the Church is both Christ's people and His Body, Christ Himself. (Indeed, St. Paul calls the Church "Christ" in 1 Cor. 12:12—not surprisingly, since it is His fullness; Eph. 1:23.) The Eucharist expresses and fulfills this identity, for the eucharistic bread represents us and our sacrifice, and it becomes Christ Himself. Also, since Christ is the Showbread, Mary is the table that holds the sacred Bread.

Before the Holy of Holies was the *golden incense-altar*. This represented the acceptability of the people's prayers to God (for which reason much incense had to be offered during the Day of Atonement sacrifices, "lest [the high-priest] die" while officiating (Lev. 16:13). Once again, the incense foreshadows Christ, the One who makes us acceptable to God. And if Christ is in the fragrant incense, Mary is the altar itself on which the incense is offered, for Christ's Incarnation depended upon her, even as the incense offering requires the altar.

In the Holy of Holies rested the *ark of the covenant*. This was the earthly locus of God's presence, for which reason it was adorned with the cherubim of glory, for just as God's heavenly court knew the presence of the angelic cherubim as guardians and servants, so the earthly locus of His presence had the carved images of the cherubim as well. Just as God's presence among men in the ark foreshadowed the Incarnation, so the ark containing God's earthly presence also foreshadowed the Mother of God, whose womb would contain the Incarnate God.

Several items rested inside the ark. First of all, it contained a *golden jar having the manna* with which God fed Israel in the days of their wandering. This also is an image of Christ, the Bread of Heaven through whom the Father gives eternal life to His people. The jar images Mary, who contained Christ and gave Him birth.

The ark also contained *the rod of Aaron that sprouted*. When Aaron's right to preside as head of the sole high-priestly family was challenged, God vindicated it through the miracle of his rod (see Num. 17). Each of the challenging tribal leaders wrote his name on his rod (the sign of his tribal authority) and, along with Aaron's rod, laid them before the Lord. The next day they found that Aaron's rod, though made of dead wood (like the other rods), nonetheless sprouted and bore buds, blossoms, and ripe almonds. That is, though dead wood, it nonetheless by the power of God brought forth life and fruit. This was the sign that God had chosen Aaron and his family to give life and spiritual fruit to Israel. Christ is the true spiritual life of His people, and He budded forth just as miraculously through the ever-virgin one. Thus Mary is the rod, Christ the fruit, and His miraculous birth from her is a sign that saving and fruitful priesthood is only through Him.

Finally, the ark contained the *tables of the covenant*, the stone tablets containing the Ten Commandments, written by the finger of God. These also foreshadow Christ. He is the timeless Word of the Father, the Father's message for all the world.

ও ও ও ও ও

6 Now when these things have been built thus, the priests are always entering the first Tent, completing the acts *of worship*,
7 but into the second *Tent* the high-priest alone *enters*, once a year, not without *taking* blood, which he offers up for himself and for the *sins of* ignorance of the people,

> 8 the Holy Spirit making plain that the way into the *Holy* of Holies has not yet been manifested, while the first Tent is still standing,
> 9 which is a parable for the present time. According *to this*, both gifts and sacrifices are offered up which are not able to make the worshipper perfect in conscience,
> 10 since they *deal* only with foods and drinks and various dippings, fleshly requirements laid on until a time of improvement.

The earthly nature of the first covenant is revealed also in how the priests used these physical arrangements. For they **are always entering the first** and outer **Tent, completing** their **acts** *of worship* (Gr. *latreias*; compare its use in v. 1). They never entered into **the second** and inner Tent. Into that Tent, **the high-priest alone** *enters*, and he only **once a year**, and even then **not without** *taking* **blood, which he offers up for himself and for the** *sins of* **ignorance of the people**. Thus even the high-priest, as a sinful man, had to atone for himself as well as for the people and so had limited access to God. (The ritual is described in detail in Lev. 16, where the rites for the Day of Atonement are prescribed.) The entire cult was arranged by God in such a way as severely to limit access into the inmost shrine, where the Presence of the God of Israel dwelt. The very fact of there being two tents—an outer and an inner one—spoke of this lack of access.

This was not accidental. Rather, it was the work of **the Holy Spirit**. That is, the Spirit who spoke in the prophets was in the Law prophetically **making plain that the way into the** *Holy* **of Holies has not yet been manifested, while the first Tent was still standing**. This, our author says, is **a parable** and a symbol (Gr. *parabole*) **for the present time**. This outer or **first Tent** represented the limit beyond which the priests, offering daily worship, could not go. They might worship in this space, but they could not go beyond it into the inner Tent. The outer Tent therefore was a symbol that access to God was restricted during this present age.

It is during this **present time** that **both** votive **gifts and sacrifices** for sins **are offered up** in that earthly shrine. These, however, **are not able to make the worshipper** who offers them **perfect in conscience**. They cannot effect inner transformation, truly removing his sins and cleansing his heart. This is because they were designed to ***deal* only with foods and drinks and various dippings, fleshly** and outer. The Law had to do with **foods and drinks** to be consumed—which foods were unclean, which were holy, which could be eaten and by whom and where (see Lev. 6:14–18; 10:9; 11)—matters that were obviously earthly and dealt with passing realities. And it dealt only with ceremonial and outer purity, such as could be obtained by **various dippings** in water to remove ritual impurity (see Lev. 14:8–9)—things that could not touch the inner heart.

Such externalism was **laid on** by God in the Law only **until a** later **time of improvement** (Gr. *diorthosis*; compare its cognate in Acts 24:2, often translated "reforms"). That is, God meant these arrangements to be provisional and temporary. They were provided to Israel only until God would bring in the final and transforming realities through Christ.

꙳ ꙳ ꙳ ꙳ ꙳

11 But when Christ appeared as a high-priest of the good things to come, *He entered* through the greater and more perfect Tent, *the one* not made with hands, that is, not of this creation,
12 and not through the blood of goats and calves, but through His own Blood, He entered the *Holy* of Holies once *for all*, having secured eternal redemption.
13 For if the blood of goats and bulls and the ashes of a heifer, sprinkling those who have been defiled, sanctify for the cleansing of the flesh,
14 how much more will the Blood of Christ, who through the eternal Spirit offered up Himself blamelessly to God, cleanse your conscience from dead works to worship the living God?

III. Christ Our High Priest   Hebrews 9:11–14

These transforming realities had now come. For **when Christ appeared as a high-priest of the good things to come** (that is, **the good things** of the Kingdom the Jewish Scriptures had prophesied), *He entered* **through the greater and more perfect Tent,** *the one* **not made with hands.** Christ did not come to exercise His priesthood in the earthly Tent, for this had to do only with the passing physical realities of this age. Christ came to bring us the eternal realities of the age to come, and so He entered into the true dwelling-place of God, *the one* **not made with** human **hands** as Moses' Tent had been—the heavenly one, **not of this creation.**

The levitical high-priest entered the earthly Holy of Holies through **the blood of goats and calves.** But not Christ. He entered the heavenly Holy of Holies **through His own Blood,** shed on the Cross. And He did not enter repeatedly, year after year, as the levitical high-priest did every Day of Atonement, but **once *for all*** (Gr. *ephapax*; compare its use in 7:27). This shedding of His Blood on the Cross effectively **secured** our **eternal redemption,** the cleansing of our sins (1:3), cleansing our hearts in a way that the levitical rites could never do, buying us back from slavery to our sins to be the free children of God.

This could be no surprise. All acknowledged that **the blood of** mere animals, **goats and bulls, and the ashes of a heifer sprinkling those who have been defiled** could indeed **sanctify** those who were ceremonially unclean **for the cleansing of** their **flesh** (see Num. 19), bringing outward ritual purity. If such things could provide outward cleansing, **how much more** would **the Blood of Christ** be able to **cleanse** the inner **conscience** from sinful **dead works** so that the worshipper could freely **worship the living God?**

For Christ's sacrifice was not like the sacrifices of animals. Such sacrifices could not provide real life, nor be in any way commensurate with the spiritual need of human beings. It is impossible that such sacrifices could deal with human sin (10:4). Only the divine life of the Son of God, **the Blood of Christ,** could avail to give life to men, for He, **through the eternal Spirit, offered up Himself to God.** And this He did **blamelessly,** offering up a sinless life, one able to cleanse us from every stain of sin. Thus His sacrifice could **cleanse**

our conscience from all defilement, fitting us to stand before God.

By saying that Christ offered Himself blamelessly **through the eternal Spirit**, our author means that Christ both lived and died by the power of the eternal Spirit of God, so that His sacrifice was made in the Spirit and thus was not bound by time and place, as merely earthly sacrifices were. Such earthly sacrifices might avail for a while but would eventually lose their potency, so that other, newer sacrifices must be offered (compare 10:1). But Christ's sacrifice would avail forever, for it was energized by the Holy Spirit, who is **eternal** and not bound or limited by the passing of time.

The word translated here *conscience* is the Greek *suneidesis*, and it means more than simply the inner faculty that makes one feel bad after sinning. It stands for the whole inner moral orientation, the heart, the sense of spiritual awareness. Christ's Blood cleanses our conscience in that it washes away guilt, renews us, and makes us radiant.

༄ ༄ ༄ ༄ ༄

15 And for this *reason* He is the mediator of a new covenant, in order that since a death happened for the redemption of transgressions *which occurred* under the first covenant, those who have been called may receive the promise of the eternal inheritance.

16 For where a covenant *is*, it is necessary for the death of the one who decreed it to be brought forward.

17 For a covenant is confirmed *only* over the dead, for it is never in force while the one who decreed it lives.

18 Therefore even the first *covenant* was not dedicated without blood.

19 For when every commandment had been spoken by Moses to all the people according to the Law, having taken the blood of the calves and the goats, with water and scarlet wool and

III. Christ Our High Priest — Hebrews 9:15–22

> hyssop, he sprinkled both the book itself and all the people,
> 20 saying, "This *is* the blood of the covenant which God commanded you."
> 21 And in the same way he sprinkled both the Tent and all the vessels of the offering-ministry with the blood.
> 22 And according to the Law, almost all things are cleansed with blood, and without blood-shedding there is no forgiveness.

Christ's priesthood, then, is rooted in His self-offering, His voluntary death on the Cross. It is because Christ has died that He is able to be **the mediator of a new covenant**. For **since His death happened for the redemption of** the **transgressions *which occurred* under the first covenant**, those who have been called through the Gospel **may** now **receive the promise of the eternal inheritance**. The death of Christ makes it possible to inherit all the things promised under the Law to the heirs of Abraham. Formerly the **transgressions *which occurred* under the first covenant** held them captive, but now, through Christ's death, there is liberation and release.

Our author illustrates the centrality of death to the new covenant by examining the word *covenant*. In Greek the word for covenant is *diatheke*, the same word used to denote a last will and testament. Our writer argues that **where a covenant** or last will and testament *is*, **it is necessary for the death of the one who decreed it to be brought forward**. That is because this **covenant** or will **is confirmed only** over the dead; **it is never in force while the one who decreed it lives**. In other words, for a will to go into effect, the one who made it must have died. This play on words in the Greek is used to illustrate the necessity of Christ's death. Just as death must occur for a will to go into effect, so Christ's death was necessary for the new covenant to go into effect.

And this is revealed typologically **even in the first *covenant*,** for it was **not dedicated** and inaugurated **without blood**. Death was a factor even in the making of the Mosaic covenant. For in Exodus 24, **when every commandment had been spoken by Moses to all the people**, Moses killed the animal sacrifices of **calves and goats**, and **having taken** their blood, along **with water and scarlet wool and hyssop, he sprinkled both the book** of the Law **itself and all the people, saying, "This *is* the blood of the covenant which God commanded you."** The death and blood of these sacrifices showed and prefigured how death is an inherent necessity in the new covenant of Christ.

Indeed, our author continues, sacrificial blood was continually necessary in the Mosaic covenant. Moses **in the same way sprinkled both the Tent and all the vessels of the offering-ministry** [Gr. *leitourgia*] **with the blood**, sprinkling the blood at the ordination of Aaron and his sons (Ex. 29) and every year afterwards on the Day of Atonement (Lev. 16). Indeed, so central is sacrificial death to union with God that according to Law, **almost all things are cleansed with blood**, for **without** such **blood-shedding there is no forgiveness** of sin. A sacrificial system in which only grain or wine was sacrificed and which offered no animals on the altar would have been recognized by all as ineffective.

> ৯৭ ৯৭ ৯৭ ৯৭ ৯৭
>
> 23 Therefore it was necessary for the models of the things in the heavens to be cleansed with these, but the heavenly things themselves with better sacrifices than these.
> 24 For Christ did not enter a *Holy* of Holies made with hands, a corresponding-pattern of the true one, but into heaven itself, now to be revealed before the face of God for us;

Thus Christ's sacrificial death is the foundation of His priesthood, and it is this death that brings cleansing to the cosmos. In the Law, in the earthly sanctuary with its altars, the **models** and copies **of the things in the heavens** were **cleansed with these** animal sacrifices. That is, the sins of men had stained the earthly sanctuary, and its altars needed sacrificial blood to atone for the sins of the worshippers and secure their access to God (such as occurred on the Day of Atonement; Lev. 16). But **the things in the heavens** themselves of which the Mosaic Tent was a model had to be cleansed **with better sacrifices than these**. Obviously animal sacrifices could not avail to secure our access to God in heaven. Animal blood might avail for earthly realities, but not for heavenly ones. Only the divine Blood of Christ could avail for that cleansing and access.

That was why **Christ did not enter a *Holy* of Holies made with hands** on earth, a perishable **corresponding-pattern of the true** heavenly Sanctuary. Rather, He entered **into heaven itself, now to be revealed** there **before the face of God for us**.

The word translated *corresponding-pattern* is the Greek *antitupos*. In the thought of Plato, the transcendent world of the ideal is contrasted to the material world of the senses, and this latter is the world of the *antitupos*, or antitype. Thus the heavenly Tabernacle is the pattern, the *tupos*, the type (see 8:5); the Mosaic Tabernacle is that **corresponding-pattern** and reflection, its *antitupos*, its antitype. And Christ entered not the earthly copy, but the heavenly original, appearing before God's holy presence on our behalf as our intercessor and sacrifice.

> ꙮ ꙮ ꙮ ꙮ ꙮ
>
> 25 nor was it that He should offer up Himself often like the high-priest *who* enters the *Holy* of Holies year by year with the blood of another,
> 26 since then He would have had to suffer often from the foundation of the world. But now once *for all* at the consummation of the ages He has been manifested to nullify sin through the sacrifice of Himself.
> 27 And inasmuch as it is laid up for men to die once *for all* and after that *comes* judgment,
> 28 thus Christ also, having been offered up once *for all* to bear the sins of many, will be seen a

> second *time* without *reference to* sin, for the salvation of those who wait for Him.

There is a final contrast to make between the two priesthoods. Not only did Christ not take the blood of goats and calves to plead before heaven as the means of our cleansing, but rather offered His own precious Blood; He also did not find it necessary to go repeatedly before God. The earthly **high-priest enters the *Holy* of Holies**, the inner shrine, **year by year with the blood of another**, striving to bring men to God. But not Christ. His one Self-offering on the Cross was sufficient. He did not need to **offer up Himself often**. It was not as if His sacrifice could avail for sins committed in the past, but not for those committed afterwards. If that were the case, **then He would have had to suffer often from the foundation of the world**, dying in each generation to save the men of that time.

The sins of the Law were indeed bound by time and could only be offered to cleanse sins already committed. But not the sacrifice of Christ. His sacrifice was eternal, availing for all the sins of men, of whatever time. So it was that in the fullness of time, **once *for all* at the consummation of all the ages**, Christ was **manifested to nullify sin through the sacrifice of Himself**. His was an eschatological offering, made once to save men of all ages.

That Christ died for sin is consistent with human life, human need, and human experience. His once-for-all death corresponds to our once-for-all deaths and is the fitting remedy to our disease. **It is laid up for men to die once *for all* and after that *comes*** the final **judgment**, when we shall stand before the Judgment Seat of Christ. Corresponding to this, Christ was **offered up once *for all*** to experience death, **to bear the sins of many**, and then He also comes to the Judgment—as our Judge! When He **will be seen a second *time***, at the Second Coming, it will be **without *reference to* sin**. He will not come then to die a second time, for like us He also was appointed to die but once. When Christ comes a second time, it will be as victorious Judge, **for the salvation of those who wait for Him**.

III. Christ Our High Priest — Hebrews 10:1–4

> ❧ ❧ ❧ ❧ ❧
>
> **10** 1 For the Law, having a shadow of the good things to come, not the very image of the things, is never able by the same sacrifices year by year, which they offer up continuously, to perfect those who come *near*.
> 2 Otherwise, would they not have ceased to be offered up because the worshipers, having once *for all* been cleansed, would no longer have a conscience of sins?
> 3 (But in those *sacrifices there is* a memorial of sins year by year.)
> 4 For it is impossible for the blood of bulls and goats to take away sins.

True and inner cleansing of sins, therefore, is only through the Blood of Christ, offered once for all (9:23–26). The sacrifices offered to God in Jerusalem cannot accomplish this. Christ's sacrifice, therefore, is not an alternative to the sacrifices of the Temple—there *is* no effectual alternative to Christ's sacrifice. That is because the Law was not meant to accomplish the inner cleansing of hearts or the transformation of human nature. It was always meant by God only as a prophecy of such work. It was not as if the levitical sacrifices were intended by God to remove sin and failed in their purpose; rather, they were never intended actually to accomplish this inner healing.

For **the Law** was only **a shadow of the good things** that would **come** in the Kingdom of God, not the very **image** and form of them (Gr. *eikon*). The contrast here is between an indistinct and hazy shadow and a clear and exact replica. Christ is elsewhere in the New Testament said to be "the image [*eikon*] of the invisible God" (Col. 1:15)—that is, the visible representation and manifestation of the invisible Father, the exact representation of His being (1:3). The word *image* is used in this sense here too: it is in Christ that **the**

good things of the Kingdom are clearly manifested. The Law was only a blurry copy of it.

Thus, the Law is **never able, by the same sacrifices** repeated **year by year** that the levitical priests **offer up continuously, to perfect** and transform **those who come** *near*. Those sacrifices express the desire of the worshipers for inner cleansing but cannot accomplish it. This is obvious. For **otherwise**, if they did accomplish it, **would** the sacrifices **not have ceased to be offered up?** If they *could* indeed **cleanse** so that the worshipers **no longer had a conscience of sins**, the worshipers would have stopped offering them. For who continues to see the physician for healing after being cured?

Here our author meditates on the frequency and multiplicity of sacrifices offered up under the Law. Sacrifices were routinely repeated again and again. At the dedication of the Temple under Solomon, for example, 22,000 peace offerings of oxen were sacrificed, as well as 120,000 sheep (1 Kin. 8:63). It is apparent that such sacrifices were never intended actually to transform human nature, but only to express the need for such transformation. The very repetitiveness of the offerings reveals that.

The sacrifices therefore constitute not a healing of sins, but rather **a memorial of sins** (Gr. *anamnesis*). The concept of memory presupposed here is not our weak modern one, but the biblical concept of God remembering and taking action (see note on 8:12). Our author makes here the bold statement that the sacrifices of the Law, far from securing cleansing from God, were simply a reminder before Him of our sins and a provocation (compare 1 Kin. 17:18). The worshiper under the Law came to the Jewish altar proclaiming his sinfulness and his need for cleansing but could not obtain it. This was not the fault of the worshiper, for it was **impossible for the blood of** mere **bulls and goats to take away sins**. The blood of livestock poured out upon an altar of stone could not change the hearts of men or give them life.

༃ ༃ ༃ ༃ ༃

5 Therefore, coming into the world, He says,
"Sacrifice and offering You have not desired,

III. Christ Our High Priest   Hebrews 10:5–9

> but a body You have prepared for Me;
> 6 "in burnt-offerings and *sacrifices* for sin You are not pleased.
> 7 "Then I said, 'Behold, I have come (in the roll of the book it is written about Me) to do Your will, O God.'"
> 8 After saying above, "Sacrifices and offerings and burnt-offerings and *sacrifices* for sin You have not desired, or been pleased with" (which are offered up according to the Law),
> 9 then He said, "Behold, I have come to do Your will." He takes away the first in order to make the second to stand.

This sanctification of human nature was to come only with the Kingdom of God and the Messiah. Once again our author proves his point by showing how this was prophesied in the Scripture. In Psalm 39:7 (LXX only), Messiah speaks to God and says, **"Sacrifice and offering You have not desired, but a body You have prepared for Me; in burnt-offerings and** *sacrifices* **for sin You are not pleased."**

In its original context, this was the prayer of a man who knows that God desires not so much animal flesh as He does the obedience of the human heart, and that without this inner love and obedience, such outward sacrifices were worthless. Our author interprets this passage messianically, as the voice of the Messiah. (Indeed, the references to enemies who seek the psalmist's life to destroy it in Psalm 39:14 support such a prophetic interpretation, as does the companion Psalm 40 with its reference to the traitor eating the psalmist's bread and then lifting up his heel against him (Ps. 40:9; John 13:18).

According to such an interpretation, these verses prophesy of Messiah's **coming into the world** through His birth from the Virgin, when God had **a body prepared** for Him. Messiah decisively comes (**Behold, I have come** has a dramatic ring to it) to **do** God's **will** for the salvation of the world. So important is this work that **in the**

roll of the book it was **written about** Him. The Book of the Law prophesied this saving messianic work.

Our author points out that such messianic salvation is deliberately contrasted in the prophetic psalm to the sacrifices of the Temple. Indeed, it is as if God intentionally sets aside such sacrifices in which He is **not pleased** in order to accept instead the work of His Messiah. For first the Messiah says, **"Sacrifices and offerings and burnt-offerings and *sacrifices* for sin You have not desired,"** and then, as if stating the alternative, He says, **"Behold, I have come to do** God's **will."** Our author sees in the long list of levitical offerings enumerated an image of the whole **Law** and concludes that this shows how the whole Mosaic dispensation is being set aside. The Messiah-psalmist here **takes away** this **first** dispensation (the Law with its offerings) **in order to make the second** dispensation **to stand**. These verses show that the first Mosaic covenant is bypassed and the new covenant under Christ is established in its place.

⚜ ⚜ ⚜ ⚜ ⚜

10 By *this* will we have been sanctified through the offering of the body of Jesus Christ once *for all*.

11 And every priest stands day by day ministering and offering up often the same sacrifices, which are never able to take away sins;

12 but this One, having offered up one sacrifice for sins forever, sat down at the right *hand* of God,

13 then to wait until His enemies are made a footstool for His feet.

14 For by one offering He has perfected forever those who are being sanctified.

Christ therefore came to do the will of the Father (v. 7), establishing a new covenant as successor to the old. And it is **by *this* will** that **we have been sanctified** and cleansed in our conscience and heart **through the offering of the body of Jesus Christ**. This

III. Christ Our High Priest — Hebrews 10:15–18

offering is again proclaimed as superior to the offerings of the Levites. For it was done **once for all** (Gr. *ephapax*), which witnesses to its effectiveness. The sacrifices of the Law were repeated time after time (vv. 1–2). Under the Law, not just the high-priest but **every priest stands** at his work, **day by day ministering** [Gr. *leitourgeo*; compare 8:6; 9:21] **and offering up often the same sacrifices**. The picture is one of unending toil. And toil that is futile, since these sacrifices **are never able to take away sins**. The levitical priest forms an image of frustration and futility.

It is otherwise with Christ. **This One** [Gr. *outos*, the emphatic form], **having offered up** but **one sacrifice for sins forever, sat down at the right hand of God**, exalted above all. The contrast could not be more stunning. The levitical priest stands because his work can never be finished nor his offerings effectual. Christ sits, for His work is fully accomplished. Now all that remains for Him is **to wait until His enemies are made a footstool for His feet**.

The reference is once again to Psalm 110:1—the very psalm that proclaimed Him to be priest forever according to the order of Melchizedek. For this is the final fruit of His priesthood—His sovereign authority as Messiah and His victory over all His foes. (There is perhaps here a latent warning to the readers of the epistle not to become Christ's **enemies** through their apostasy.) Christ can wait at the Father's right hand in serene repose, **for by one offering**, once made at the Cross, **He has perfected forever those who are being sanctified** and cleansed. (The word *sanctified*—Gr. *agiazo*—refers to the cleansing of the heart, one's forgiveness and transformation in Christ. It is not used merely to denote an improvement in behavior but as a synonym for our washing and justification and forgiveness; see a similar use in 1 Cor. 6:11.) Becoming a Christian involves a permanent and decisive inner cleansing of the heart and conscience (compare Acts 15:9).

ॐ ॐ ॐ ॐ ॐ

15 And the Holy Spirit also witnesses to us; for after saying,

> 16 "This *is* the covenant that I will decree for them after those days, says the Lord: I will put My laws upon their hearts and upon their mind I will write them," *He then says,*
> 17 "and their sins and their lawless *acts* I will *certainly* not remember any longer."
> 18 Now where there is forgiveness of these things, *there is* no longer an offering for sin.

Our author once again refers to his Scripture text in Jeremiah 31:33–34, already mentioned in 8:8–12. He refers to this text as **the Holy Spirit witnessing to us**—that is, as a prophecy of Christian salvation. **For after saying, "This *is* the covenant that I will decree for them; I will put My laws upon their hearts,"** the Spirit then says through Jeremiah, **"their sins and their lawless *acts* I will *certainly* not remember any longer."**

Our author points out that this new covenant involves a transformation of the heart (**"I will put My laws upon their hearts"**) in which God does **not remember any longer** the people's **sins and lawless acts**. What can this mean, our author says, but that the problem of sin has been effectively dealt with? Christ's one sacrifice accomplished the **forgiveness of these things**, cleansing the heart from these **sins and lawless acts**. Therefore *there is* **no longer an offering for sin**, for there is no longer any need for it. The prophecy in Jeremiah 31 that God would no longer remember sin is a further witness that Christ's high-priesthood does not involve repeated offerings for sin, but that our iniquities would be cleansed by a single, eternal offering.

❧ EXCURSUS:
On the Sacrifice of Christ and on the Eucharist

The sacrifice of Christ upon the Cross was not only an historical event, it was also an eschatological event. That is, Christ sacrificed Himself to God "through the eternal Spirit"

(9:14), and this once-for-all and unrepeatable sacrifice took away the sins of the world (7:27).

The Church has always understood her Eucharist to be a sacrifice (compare the reference to the Eucharist simply as "your sacrifice" in the *Didache*, chapter 14, dating from about AD 100). In fact, the Church has understood the Eucharist to be identical with the sacrifice of Christ and speaks of the celebrant as "offering" the eucharistic oblation to God (for example, Clement of Rome's Epistle to the Corinthians, chapter 44, dated about AD 95). This sacrificial vocabulary regarding the Eucharist persists in the Church's Liturgy to this day. How can all this be reconciled to the teaching in our epistle that Christ's sacrifice is unique and unrepeatable?

It is important to understand not only what the Church teaches on this subject but also what it does not teach. The Church does *not* teach that Christ dies afresh or is offered afresh at every Eucharist, undergoing again the rigors of Golgotha at every Liturgy. Such a teaching would indeed contradict the Epistle to the Hebrews. But that is not the Church's understanding of the eucharistic sacrifice.

The Church teaches that her Eucharist is sacrificial in that it is a "rational and bloodless worship," a sacrifice that is not physical, but rational, noetic, spiritual (Gr. *logiken kai anaimokton latreian*). More specifically, it is an *anamnesis* or memorial before God of the sacrifice of Christ, and it is in this effectual memorial that the unique and eternal sacrifice of Christ is present in our midst.

Christ remains in heaven before the Father as our intercessor. That is, He abides before God as the Lamb slain (Rev. 5:6), as the eternal sacrifice, and this sacrificial presence is eternally effective. It is this presence that we remember and plead before God in the Eucharist and thereby make effectively present for ourselves now in our midst.

As St. John Chrysostom said (in his Sermon 17 on

Hebrews), "We ever offer the same Person, not today one Lamb and tomorrow another, but the same offering. . . . We offer now that which was then offered [by Christ], which cannot be exhausted. This is done for a memorial of that which was then done. . . . We do not offer another sacrifice [than Christ offered] but we ever offer the same; for rather, we make memorial of the sacrifice."

Christ's heavenly high-priesthood is fulfilled in the royal priesthood of the Church (compare 1 Pet. 2:9), and we access His sacrifice through our eucharistic Liturgy. It is only because He is our high-priest that His Body, the Church, is a corporate priesthood, and that her presbyters serve as priests.

Christ is present within the veil, in the heavenly Holy of Holies, as our saving Eucharist. It is through His presence before the Father that we on earth draw near to God to find our needed cleansing and grace, our continual perfecting and ongoing healing and transformation.

❧ IV ❧

HOLD FAST TO CHRIST
(10:19—12:29)

Having shown at length how Christ is a true high-priest in heaven and is far superior to the levitical priests on earth, our author applies these lessons. If Christ is indeed such a priest, let the readers of the epistle hold fast to Him! Let them not drift away from their allegiance to Christ and fall back into Judaism, relying on an inferior and obsolete dispensation. For if they do this, there will be no forgiveness for them on the Last Day. As true members of the holy nation of Israel, let them imitate their fathers in olden days and hold fast to their faith, looking to the final reward.

§IV.1. Do Not Draw Back from Christian Worship (10:19–39)

> 19 Therefore brothers, having boldness to enter the *Holy* of Holies by the Blood of Jesus,
> 20 by a recent and living way which He dedicated for us through the curtain, that is, His flesh,
> 21 and *since we have* a great priest over the House of God,
> 22 let us come *near* with a true heart in full-assurance of faith, having our hearts sprinkled *clean* from a conscience of evil and our bodies washed with clean water.

He begins first by addressing them once more as **brothers**—brothers not only of one another, but also of Christ, since they have become partakers of a heavenly calling (3:1), and now have

boldness through Christ **to enter the *Holy* of Holies** in heaven **by the Blood of Jesus**. Christ's dispensation or divine plan is called the **recent and living way which He dedicated** or inaugurated **for us through the curtain**.

Once again, our author draws upon the levitical images he has been using (compare 9:11–12). As the levitical high-priest entered the earthly Holy of Holies, bringing with him the blood of another (9:7), so Christ entered the presence of God in heaven, offering His own Blood. The earthly priest had to pass through a curtain of physical fabric; Christ had to pass through the barrier of death, in which it was not a veil that was opened, but **His** own **flesh** that was pierced. This way of access to God is called **recent** because Christ had just opened this way within recent memory; it is called **living** because Christ lives forever to guarantee our access to God.

Since this is so, and ***we have*** a **great** and exalted **priest over the House of God**, the family of faith (3:6), all the readers must **come *near*** to God in the Church's Liturgy, having **a true heart**. That is, they must remain loyal to Christ and resist the insidious and cancerous growth within them of an evil heart of unbelief (3:12). They may come near in **full-assurance of faith**, confident of God's welcome and help. This they could do, for their hearts were **sprinkled *clean* from a conscience of evil** and their **bodies** were **washed with clean water**.

The image here is drawn once more from the levitical requirements for worship. In Numbers 19, rules are given for purifying ritual uncleanness; these include being sprinkled with sacrificial ashes and having one's body and clothes washed with water. After such washing, one must wait until evening. Only then could the cleansed one draw near to God to worship before His altar.

Analogously, the Christian now is cleansed and can draw near to God in heaven through Christ. But it is not his outer form that is **sprinkled *clean***, but his inner **conscience** that is cleansed from **evil**. He does not wash his body and wait until evening to be ritually cleansed. Rather, his body is **washed with clean water** in Holy Baptism, and he is even then able to draw near and call on the Name of the Lord (Acts 22:16).

IV. Hold Fast to Christ — Hebrews 10:23–25

> ⚜ ⚜ ⚜ ⚜ ⚜
> 23 Let us hold fast the confession of hope unwaveringly, for He who promised is faithful,
> 24 and let us consider how to incite one another to love and good works,
> 25 not leaving behind the gathering together of ourselves, as is the custom of some, but encouraging *one another*, and all the more as you see the Day drawing near.

Given these privileges, they must **hold fast the confession of hope unwaveringly**. They must never let their **confession** of faith in Jesus falter, for this is their **hope** of salvation. Whatever opposition they encounter, they must persevere. Such perseverance will be worthwhile because **He who promised** that salvation to them **is faithful** and will fulfill His promise.

For their part, let them **consider how to incite** and provoke **one another to love and good works**. The word translated *incite* is the Greek *paroxusmos*, translated as "provocation" where it is used in a negative sense (compare our English "paroxysm"). Our author here is perhaps gently chiding his readers for their past quarrels (later he will exhort them to "pursue peace with everyone," 12:14), and encouraging them to exchange a negative spirit of competition for a positive one. In the past they competed to get the better of one another; now let them compete to help one another do better! Let them now **encourage** *one another* and exhort one another to walk in **love** and excel in **good works** of charity and service. And let them do this **all the more as** they **see the Day** of Judgment **drawing** ever more **near** each day. There was no time to lose!

These instructions presupposed that they did not abandon or **leave behind** their **gathering together** each Sunday in eucharistic assembly. It was **the custom of some** to abandon Christian worship, and such a lapse was disastrous. All their life together as Christians was built on the foundation of their weekly **gathering together** as the Body of Christ. If they lost this, they lost everything. Some of their Jewish Christian friends had already fallen away from Christ and contented themselves with attendance at synagogue and Temple, thinking this would prove sufficient.

> ৩ ৩ ৩ ৩ ৩
>
> 26 For if we sin voluntarily, after receiving the real-knowledge of the truth, there is no longer left a sacrifice for sin,
> 27 but a certain fearful expectation of judgment and a jealous fire which is about to eat up the adversaries.
> 28 Anyone who has nullified the Law of Moses dies without compassion on *the word* of two or three witnesses.
> 29 How much worse punishment do you think he will be counted worthy of who has trampled on the Son of God, and has esteemed as unclean the blood of the covenant by which he was sanctified, and has insulted the Spirit of grace?
> 30 For we know Him who said, "Mine is the avenging, I *Myself* will render!" And again, "The Lord will judge His people."
> 31 It is a fearful *thing* to fall into the hands of the living God.

It was not sufficient. Our author solemnly warns his readers that if they continue to **sin voluntarily after receiving the real-knowledge of the truth**, there will **no longer** be **left** for them any **sacrifice for sin**. Their offerings in the Temple will avail them nothing on the Last Day. Instead, there is **a certain fearful expectation of judgment and a jealous fire which** is **about to eat up** God's **adversaries**. This is to be their lot if they fall from Christ and His Church!

The words *sin voluntarily* need to be understood in context. The verb is in the present tense, indicating an ongoing and habitual action. It is sometimes translated as "if we go on sinning" (NASB),

IV. Hold Fast to Christ   Hebrews 10:26-31

"if we persist in sin" (NEB). The thought is not of the occasional sin that entangles the steps of all; it is of the self-chosen sin of continued apostasy. This is clear from the word *voluntarily*, sometimes rendered "willfully, deliberately, intentionally" (Gr. *ekousios*). The thought here is of "sinning with a high hand" (see Num. 15:30), of defiantly rejecting God and His covenant. After such apostasy from **the truth** of Christ, the sacrifice offered in the Temple is useless to save. One's only **expectation** and prospect is for **judgment**.

This judgment is further described as **a jealous fire which is about to eat up the adversaries**. The phrase rendered *a jealous fire* is actually rendered more literally as "a jealousy of fire" (Gr. *puros zelos*). It is a reference to Isaiah 26:11 in the Septuagint Greek, which reads, "jealousy shall seize an untaught people . . . fire shall consume the adversaries." In its original context, it refers to God's jealous judgment on His people for their sins (see also Deut. 5:9). Our author applies this notion of God jealously judging His people for their betrayal of His love to those who apostatize from Christ, and assures his readers that this fate awaits them too if they turn away from the Lord.

This is only fair. For **anyone who has nullified** and decisively rejected **the Law of Moses dies without compassion on *the word of two or three witnesses***. That is, in the Law, if one apostatized from the Mosaic covenant and turned away from the living God to worship idols, one was executed **without compassion** if only **two or three witnesses** would testify that one had in fact worshipped the idols (Deut. 17:2–6). This was acknowledged as fair by all pious Jews.

Therefore, **how much worse punishment** did they think one could be **counted worthy of** who apostatized from the superior new covenant of Christ? For such an apostate had by his apostasy **trampled on the** very **Son of God** Himself and had **esteemed as unclean** and common **the blood of the** new **covenant**, declaring by his apostasy that Christ did not shed His Blood and die as a holy sacrifice, but as a common guilty criminal. How horrible—since it was this same holy Blood **by which he was sanctified** by baptism and Eucharist. Indeed, he had **insulted the Spirit** of God who had once offered him **grace** and forgiveness, blaspheming the Holy Spirit by turning against Jesus and siding with His foes (compare Mark 3:29–30).

No doubt the one apostatizing from Christ did not see his actions in this light. As far as he was concerned, he was not apostatizing from Christ at all, but simply pulling back a bit from certain Christian practices, such as attendance at the weekly Eucharist and public confession of Jesus as Messiah. Our author, however, is concerned to portray these actions in their true light and to ascribe to them their true and full significance. The retreat from public confession of Jesus and withdrawal from the Church was in reality an apostasy from Christ, and would be treated by God as such. Let any contemplating such a course of action take heed!

For they all **knew Him who said** in the Scriptures, **"Mine is the avenging, I Myself will render!" and again** (repeating the warning with another scriptural citation lest there be any mistake), **"The Lord will judge His people"** (Deut. 32:35, 36). That God would judge Israel's sins was no novel concept to them. He had told Israel this repeatedly in the Scriptures (Ps. 50:22; 51:4; Ezek. 18:30), and they knew that it was **a fearful *thing*** for the defiant rebel **to fall into the hands of the living** and avenging **God**. There was thus no excuse for apostasy and sin, and no favoritism or partiality. God was the righteous Judge, the One who would vindicate the righteous and destroy the impenitent faithless.

❦ EXCURSUS
On the Wrath of God

Throughout the epistle, the author urges his readers to remember the wrath of God reserved for rebels and apostates. This concept, so thoroughly biblical that it is found from one end of Scripture to the other (see Gen. 3:22–24; Rev. 6:16; 22:18–19), has become unpalatable to modern readers. Our spiritual forebears had no such scruples. It is only in modern times that we have come to regard the idea of God having wrath at human sin as problematic, if not downright repugnant. I suspect that this is because our generation is unique in having lost a sense of sin. As C. S. Lewis wrote in 1948, "[There is in modern times] the almost total absence from the minds of [people] of any sense of sin . . . the ancient man approached God (or even the gods) as the accused person approaches his judge. For the modern man the roles are reversed. He is the judge: God is in the dock."[1]

Nonetheless, the Epistle to the Hebrews remains incomprehensible without this concept, for it is replete with warnings against apostasy. Consider the following citations: "How shall we escape if we neglect so great a salvation?" (2:3). "Let us be afraid lest, while a promise remains of entering into His rest, any one of you should seem to have come short of it" (4:1). "If [the ground] yields thorns and thistles, it is worthless and near to a curse; and its end is for burning" (6:8). "If we sin voluntarily there is . . . a certain fearful expectation of judgment, and a jealous fire which is about to consume the adversaries . . . it is a fearful thing to fall into the hands of the living God" (10:26–27, 31). "If they did not escape when they rejected Him who warned on earth, much less shall we who turn away from Him who warns from the heavens . . . for our God is a consuming fire" (12:25, 29).

Behind all the arguments, teachings, typology, and exhortations of the epistle stands the possibility of the readers falling from the Faith and enduring God's wrath. The thought of inheriting God's Kingdom is incentive to persevere; the thought of inheriting His wrath is dissuasive from apostasy. As St. Paul wrote, we must behold both "the kindness and severity of God" (Rom. 11:22) and not dismiss His severity because we moderns find it unpalatable.

How can we, whose culture blinds us to the justice of

---

[1] C. S. Lewis, "God in the Dock," in *God in the Dock*, ed. Walter Hooper (Grand Rapids, MI: Eerdmans Publishing Company, 1970), pp. 243–244.

God's wrath against sin, come to terms emotionally with this biblical concept? It is a long and difficult business to overcome one's cultural conditioning. But one thought may be helpful. The one time many of us have no problem with the thought of God's wrath against sin (that is, our own sin) is when our conscience smites us. Most of the time we go about our daily business with a clear conscience (whether we deserve such a clear conscience or not). But on occasion, we do something terribly wrong, and our conscience rebukes us. We feel ashamed, dirty, unworthy.

This is, I suggest, a rare glimpse into our true state, into what God and His angels see in us all the time. In these moments, the wrath of God against our sin does not appear to be unwarranted, unfair, or unworthy of Him. It appears to us to be what it is: the just response of goodness when confronted with moral evil. Goodness must view such depravity as repugnant, or it would not be true goodness. When our conscience condemns us, we realize this truth, if only fleetingly. This realization may help act as a corrective to the lack of consciousness of sin our modern culture has bred into us.

※ ※ ※ ※ ※

32 But remember the former days when, after being enlightened, you endured a great contest of sufferings,
33 sometimes by being made a spectacle through reproaches and tribulations, and sometimes by becoming sharers with those who were thus treated.
34 For you *showed* sympathy to the prisoners and

IV. Hold Fast to Christ   Hebrews 10:32–36

> welcomed with joy the seizure of your possessions, knowing that you have for yourselves a better possession and an abiding one.
> 35 Therefore do not cast away your boldness, which has a great recompense.
> 36 For you have need of perseverance, so that having done the will of God, you may receive back the promise.

Our author continues to encourage his readers to persevere, reminding them of the great reward their past faithfulness had won for them. They were doing so well—let them not give up now! Surely they could **remember the former days** as new converts **when, after being enlightened** in Holy Baptism, they **endured a great contest of sufferings**. The word rendered *contest* is the Greek *athlesis* (cognate with the verb *athleo*; compare the verb's use in 2 Tim. 2:5). The English word "athlete" is derived from this. These Hebrew Christians had proven themselves great spiritual athletes by the suffering and persecution they endured.

Sometimes they were **made a spectacle**, when they were subjected to public **reproaches** and insults and other **tribulations** (possibly such as being beaten or imprisoned). **Sometimes** they *showed* **sympathy to the prisoners** who had suffered by visiting them and thus **became sharers with those who were thus treated**. When their public loyalty to Jesus Christ and His disciples cost them their **possessions** (possibly plundered while they were imprisoned?), they **welcomed with joy** this **seizure** of their property. They were content to let it all go, **knowing that** they **had** for themselves **a better possession and an abiding one**—wealth in heaven that no one could plunder.

Their **boldness** in proclaiming their faith in Jesus was about to bring **a great recompense**—let them **not cast away** such triumphant faith. They were doing wonderfully—they just **had need of**

perseverance so that they could continue to **do the will of God** by holding to their faith. Then they would **receive back the promise** of final salvation (compare 6:12).

> ༄ ༄ ༄ ༄ ༄
> 37 For "yet in a little while, the coming one will come and will not delay.
> 38 "But My righteous one will live by faith, and if he shrinks back, My soul is not pleased with him."
> 39 But we *ourselves* are not of those who shrink back to destruction, but of those who have faith to the acquisition of the soul.

The exhortation is crowned with another quote from Scripture. In the Greek of Habakkuk 2:3–4 (somewhat different from the Hebrew), God says, **"the coming one will come and will not delay. But My righteous one will live by faith, and if he shrinks back, My soul is not pleased with him."** **The coming one** was identified with the Messiah (indeed, "He Who Comes" was a messianic title; see Matt. 11:3; John 11:27). His Second Coming to judge would surely **come** and **not delay**. All might be sure that the final Judgment would come. Meanwhile, God's **righteous one**, His follower, was to **live by faith**, persevering in his faithfulness and not shrinking back from commitment to His Messiah. For if that righteous one *did* **shrink back**, God's **soul** would be **not pleased with him**. That is, when the Coming One would finally come, God would repudiate the apostate.

Our author hastens to assure his readers that he does not think they have this dire fate in store for them. He is not mentioning such terrible wrath because he thinks this is what awaits them. On the contrary, their faith would bring them a great recompense and reward (v. 35). They were **not of those who shrink back** from faith **to** their final **destruction**. Their hearts were not yet evil hearts of unbelief (3:12). Their hearts were true (10:22); they were **of those who have faith**, so that they would finally attain to **the acquisition** and preservation **of** their **soul**. God had promised in Habakkuk 2 that the one who had **faith** would **live**, and their unwavering faith in Jesus would result in eternal life in the Kingdom of God.

§IV.2. Hold Fast to Faith as the Fathers Did (11:1—12:2)

> ॐ ॐ ॐ ॐ ॐ
>
> **11** 1 Now faith is the conviction of things hoped for, the proof of things not seen.
> 2 For by it the elders were witnessed to.
> 3 By faith we understand that the ages were prepared by the word of God, so that the *things which are* seen did not come to exist from *things which are* visible.

Reference in 10:38–39 to **faith** as the essential ingredient in saving perseverance leads our author to show the role of faith in Israel's history. By doing so, he strives to inspire his readers to imitate those who through faith and patience would inherit the promise of final salvation (6:12). If they would hold fast to their faith, they would be true Israelites indeed, following in the footsteps of their illustrious forebears. These men and women lived their whole lives relying on nothing more tangible than God's promise and word, and it is to this example that the Christians were now called. Now is the time of faith—the divine reward will come later.

For **faith**, by its very nature, is faith in what cannot yet be seen or seized upon—it is faith of a *future* reward. That is, it **is the conviction of things hoped for** in the future, **the proof of** realities **not** yet **seen**. To have the saving faith referred to in Habakkuk 2:4 is, of necessity, to have firm trust in a reality as yet intangible. It is **by** this faith that **the elders**, the heroes of Israel's sacred history, **were witnessed to** (Gr. *martureo*; cognate with *martus*, witness). It is through their faith that they received testimony from God and gained His approval.

Our author begins by saying that they already held to such faith simply by being Jews. For as Jews, they believed that God created the world out of nothing. Indeed, adherence to this dogma was part of what made one a Jew. Thus they held to the **conviction** about **things not seen** already, and he was not calling them to anything foreign or strange. For they believed that the visible world was created out of **things not seen**—namely, the invisible and intangible creative words of God. It was His primordial utterance that built the cosmos. He merely said, "Let there be light!" and there was light. Thus, all the world with its **ages** (Gr. *aion*), all that existed and would come to be, **were prepared by the word of God**, by God's simple word of command.

But it is **by faith that we understand** this. For the unspiritual and faithless man cannot fathom how such a thing could be—how things that were **seen** and tangible **did not come to exist from** physical ***things which are* visible**. This seemed like folly to him, for how (he reasoned) could something be formed from nothing? Faith alone enabled one to grasp this insight—even as faith alone would enable one to seize the intangible realities still to come.

༄ ༄ ༄ ༄ ༄

4 By faith Abel offered up to God a greater sacrifice than Cain, through which he was witnessed to as being righteous, God witnessing to his gifts, and through it, though he is dead, he still speaks.

5 By faith Enoch was removed so as not to see death; and he was not found because God removed him; for he was witnessed to that before his removal he was pleasing to God.

6 And without faith it is impossible to please *Him*, for it is necessary for the one who comes *near* to God to have faith that He is, and that He becomes a recompensor of the ones seeking Him out.

IV. Hold Fast to Christ — Hebrews 11:4–6

Our author begins his survey of salvation history with **Abel**, showing that it was **by faith** that he **offered up to God a greater sacrifice than** his brother **Cain** (Gen. 4:1–5). That is, righteous Abel was acceptable to God because of his faith. Cain was unrighteous and sinned in making his offering. Sin strove for mastery over him and achieved that mastery—for out of envy of his righteous brother, Cain finally rose up and killed him (Gen. 4:6f). Abel's sacrifice, therefore, was greater than Cain's because it came from faith. Abel approached God in humility, offering what he had from a heart of devotion, trusting that God would accept his offering, even though he had no proof that He would do so. And God indeed **witnessed to** him **as being righteous** and acceptable to Him by **witnessing to his gifts**—that is (we may suppose), by sending fire from heaven to consume the offering on the altar, as He did in the time of Elijah (1 Kin. 18:38). As said above, Cain responded to this by killing his brother, and Abel's blood cried to God from the ground for justice (Gen. 4:10). Indeed, says our author, even **though** Abel is **dead**, that righteous blood **still speaks** from the ground, for not only did it cry out for justice, but it continues even now to proclaim his righteousness and the necessity of faith—which faith is stronger even than murder and death.

Another hero who lived before the Flood was Enoch (Gen. 5:24). He too was righteous and "was pleasing to God" (Gen. 5:24 LXX). This faithful man **was removed so as not to see death**, **and he was not found** on the earth **because God removed him**. The idea here is of Enoch being bodily taken by God to Paradise, as Elijah also was (2 Kin. 2:11). This interpretation of the Genesis account was common in Israel and can be found in Sirach 44:16. For our author, Enoch's removal gives the proof of Enoch's faith. **Before his removal**, Enoch **was pleasing to God**, and his removal **witnessed to** this fact.

Both Abel and Enoch lived lives pleasing to God through their faith, but they did not have the proof of this until later—Abel, until God accepted his gifts; Enoch, until God removed him from this mortal realm. They both persevered in their faith, continuing in the absence of tangible proof that God would reward them.

What then did these two examples prove? That **without faith** [Gr. *pistis*] **it is impossible to please** God (Gr. *euaresteo*; compare its use in Gen. 5:24 LXX to describe Enoch). Indeed, **it is necessary for the one who comes *near* to God** (as Abel did through his sacrifice, and as Enoch did when He was removed) **to have faith** (Gr. *pisteuo*) **that He is, and that He becomes a recompensor of the ones seeking Him out.** That is, one must not only believe that God exists. One must also believe that He will **become** one's **recompensor** (Gr. *misthapodotes*), the One who will one day bestow one's hoped-for recompense (Gr. *misthapodosia*; compare its use in 10:35). Abel and Enoch served God with faith and only later received their reward. It is to be the same with us: we also serve God and look to a future salvation. To approach God, therefore, of necessity involves faith in a future and as-yet-unrealized reward. Without such persevering faith, **it is impossible to please *Him*.** Those who cast away their faith will have no reward or salvation on the Last Day.

> ৯৭ ৯৭ ৯৭ ৯৭ ৯৭
>
> 7 By faith Noah, being warned about things not yet seen, having become reverent, built an ark for the salvation of his house, by which he condemned the world and became an heir of the righteousness which is according to faith.

This principle of faith in a future reward is seen preeminently in the life of **Noah** (Gen. 6–9). He was **warned** by God **about things not yet seen**—namely, the coming Flood that would destroy the earth. Noah had **become reverent** and pious (Gr. *eulabetheis*; compare the use of its cognate *eulabeia* in Heb. 5:7 and 12:28). That is, he had achieved a state in which he was faithful and submissive, a single shining light in a dark world. It was because of his submissiveness to God that he obeyed His word and **built an ark for the salvation of his house.** By doing this he condemned the world, proving wrong their scorn for his preaching and their rejection of his God. More than this, he **became an heir of the righteousness** and vindication **which is according to faith.** God vindicated him when the waters

IV. Hold Fast to Christ   Hebrews 11:8–12

of the Flood drowned the world. Noah had proclaimed to all that the Flood would come and that all should repent, but they rejected his preaching. Now he was proven right, and he and his family alone escaped the catastrophe and inherited a renewed world.

This was all **according to faith**, and this proves what the lives of Abel and Enoch do also—that faith involves persevering to receive a later reward. Noah received the reward of his faith, but he received it *as an inheritance*—as something he would receive only later, after the Flood. Until that time, he had to believe in things only "hoped for," in "things not seen" (11:1).

> ༃ ༃ ༃ ༃ ༃
>
> 8 By faith Abraham, being called, obeyed and went out to a place which he was about to receive for an inheritance; and he went out, not understanding where he was going.
> 9 By faith he sojourned in *the* land of the promise as in another land, dwelling in tents with Isaac and Jacob, co-heirs of the same promise;
> 10 for he was waiting for the city which has foundations, whose builder and craftsman is God.
> 11 By faith even Sarah herself, a barren *woman*, received power to conceive, even beyond the time of age, since she esteemed Him faithful who had promised.
> 12 Therefore also there was born from one *person*, and him *become* dead, as *many descendants* as the stars of heaven in multitude and innumerable as the sand by the shore of the sea.

After these early examples of faith, our author turns to the supreme architects of the Jewish faith, Abraham, Isaac, Jacob, and Moses. They too were paradigms of faith; their lives too revealed the need to persevere for an as-yet-unrealized recompense.

Abraham, being called by God, **obeyed** that call **and went out** from Ur of the Chaldees **to a place which he was about to receive**

for an inheritance (Gen. 12:1f). He was so far from receiving this inheritance that **he went out not** even **understanding where he was going**. God called him simply to go out and follow what directions he was to be given, and he journeyed forth, ignorant of his final destination. **He sojourned in *the* land of promise**, living there as an exile and a stranger, **as in another land**. Even though this was the land God had promised him he would inherit, he dwelt there as if it were a foreign land that he had not been promised. He did not build a house, as he would have if he considered himself a permanent settler there. Rather, he continued in his nomadic existence, **dwelling in tents with Isaac and Jacob,** who were **co-heirs of the same promise**.

For Abraham and his heirs were not simply émigrés. Abraham was not simply looking for a place in which to settle. He was following God, thirsting after something the world could not provide. He was **waiting for the city which has** lasting and eternal **foundations, whose builder and craftsman is God**. All cities on earth were settled and built by someone. But Abraham was not seeking such a dwelling place. His heart was restless for a peace earth could not afford; his eyes were focused on a destination beyond earthly horizons. Cynical men would call him a dreamer. Wiser men would call him a visionary. Christian men knew that he was seeking for the Kingdom, and that he was called to find his home among men of whom the world was not worthy.

Even Sarah herself, a barren *woman*, shared that calling, although the promises were not made to her but to her husband. She **received power to conceive** (literally, "for the foundation of seed"), **even beyond the time of age** when women could conceive (Gen. 17:15f; 21:1f). This was **by faith** and through the miraculous power of God, **since she esteemed** God **faithful who had promised**. Once again, she believed God would fulfill His promise in the future, despite all her experience, which said women of her age could not conceive. **Therefore also there was born from one *person*,** from Abraham, and him *become* **dead** as far as normal child-rearing was concerned, **as *many descendants* as the stars**

of heaven in multitude (Gen. 22:17). The one became the many through the power of faith.

> 13 All these died in faith, not having received the promises, but having seen them and having greeted them from a distance, and having confessed that they were strangers and exiles on the earth.
> 14 For those who say such things reveal that they are seeking after a homeland.
> 15 And indeed, if they had been remembering that *one* from which they went out, they would have had opportunity to turn back.
> 16 But as it is, they aspire to a better *homeland*, that is, a heavenly *one*. Therefore God is not *at all* ashamed to be called upon *as* their God; for He has prepared for them a city.

What did the examples of these patriarchs mean? That having faith means persevering throughout this earthly life, seeking for a reward not of this world. For **all these** patriarchs **died in faith, not having received the promises** God made to them. God promised them something (a homeland, an innumerable progeny), but they did not receive the fulfillment of these promises in their lifetime. Rather, they **greeted** these promises **from a distance**, seeing them from afar. They **confessed** by their lives **that they were strangers and exiles on the earth**, and that this age was not their true home.

Our author makes his meaning clearer, saying that **those who say such things** about being an exile **are seeking after a homeland**. When one confesses oneself to be in exile, one longs for home and admits that every place one stays is only a temporary lodging. For most such earthly exiles, that homeland is on earth, and they were driven from it by war or some other catastrophe. As soon as circumstances permit, those exiles will return home.

It is otherwise with the patriarchs. **If they had been remembering that** homeland **from which they went out** (such as Ur of the Chaldees), **they would have had opportunity to turn back** to it. But when Abraham and his heirs confessed by their lives and their wanderings that they were exiles, they were not longing to return to Ur. Rather, **they aspired to a better *homeland*** than this age could afford, **that is, a heavenly *one***. Because of their visionary desire to dwell with God, He **is not *at all* ashamed to be called upon *as* their** God. That is, God is content to be identified with such as these and to be for later ages invoked as the God of Abraham and Isaac and Jacob. Moreover, He will fulfill their aspiration and **has prepared for them a city**—the eternal city of God in the age to come. Throughout their lives, their desire was not fulfilled. But God was faithful, and He would fulfill their desires in the coming Kingdom. The examples of the patriarchs proved that faith by definition looks to a final and future reward.

ও৴ ও৴ ও৴ ও৴ ও৴

17 By faith Abraham, when he was tested, offered up Isaac; and he who had accepted the promises was offering up his only-begotten,

18 about whom it was spoken, "In Isaac will your seed be called."

19 He reckoned that God is even able to raise from the dead, from which he also received him back as a parable.

20 By faith Isaac blessed Jacob and Esau, even about coming *things*.

21 By faith Jacob, when dying, blessed each of the sons of Joseph and worshipped upon the top of his staff.

22 By faith Joseph, when he was ending, reminded *them* about the exodus of the sons of Israel and commanded about his bones.

IV. Hold Fast to Christ   Hebrews 11:17–22

That faith presupposes a future reward was seen not just by the wanderings of the patriarchs but also in their other experiences as well. **Abraham** not only sojourned as an exile in the Promised Land, waiting for the future fulfillment of God's promises, but also, **when he was tested** by God, he **offered up Isaac**. The full account of the story is found in Genesis 22. God tested Abraham's willingness to obey Him by commanding him to offer up in sacrifice **his only-begotten,** his darling Isaac, **about whom it was spoken** by God, **"In Isaac will your seed be called"** (Gen. 21:12). (Isaac is called **only-begotten** because of his unique status, which his brother Ishmael did not share.) That is, it was through Isaac that Abraham would have descendants; it was through him that all God's promises to Abraham would be fulfilled. In sacrificing Isaac, therefore, Abraham was sacrificing all his future hopes.

This offering of Isaac, when Abraham took him to the top of Mount Moriah, bound him, and raised high the sacrificial knife to slay him, was the supreme example of Abraham's trust in God. It was indeed **by faith** that he offered him up, for he was prepared to slay his son in the confidence that God would fulfill His word to give him sons through Isaac, even if it meant that He would **raise** Isaac **from the dead**. For in Genesis 22:5, Abraham tells his companions that he and his son will go up Mount Moriah to worship *and come again to them*. That is, Abraham expected he would return with Isaac, even if that meant a return from death, for **God** was **able** to conquer even death and would do so to keep His promise.

Thus, when God stayed Abraham's hand and kept him from slaying his son (Gen. 22:10f), so that Isaac did indeed return with Abraham, this formed a **parable**, a type and image (Gr. *parabole*) of the Resurrection of Christ, the true Only-begotten of the Father. Our author mentions this in passing. His main point is that Abraham offered up Isaac in faith, looking to a future fulfillment of God's word to him, even if this involved conquering death.

This future-looking faith in God was reproduced in his heirs also. **By faith Isaac blessed Jacob and Esau** in his old age (Gen. 27:27f, 39f). That is, he invoked the blessing and will of God upon them as his final legacy. And he spoke not just about present things, such as the distribution of his possessions in a kind of last will and testament. He also spoke **about coming *things***, invoking (or withholding) future blessings from God, trusting that God would fulfill his word and will for his sons even after he had died.

By faith Jacob, too, **when dying blessed each of the sons of Joseph**, Ephraim and Manasseh (Gen. 48). By this blessing, he too invoked God's will upon the boys, giving the preeminence to the younger Ephraim and not to the elder Manasseh (Gen. 48:14f). This was contrary to the custom of those days, which gave preeminence to the elder. But Jacob insisted on giving preeminence to the younger, prophesying a greater destiny for him and expecting God to fulfill his prophetic word. Moreover, though on his deathbed, when he **worshipped** God, he leaned **upon the top of his staff** (Gen. 47:31 LXX; the Masoretic says he leaned on the top of his *bed*), as if to stress that he still lived as a pilgrim and would keep close to him the pilgrim staff as a wanderer on the earth.

By faith Joseph as well, **when he was ending** his life, **reminded** his sons **about the** coming **exodus of the sons of Israel** (Gen. 50:24–25). He knew from his father and grandfather that God had sworn to give the land of Palestine, the land of Abraham's sojourning, to their descendants, and that God would keep His word. He therefore **commanded** his sons **about his bones**, charging them to take his earthly remains with them when God brought them out of Egypt into Palestine and to bury his bones there.

Thus all the patriarchs looked to God in faith, trusting that God would fulfill His word in the future and even after their deaths.

☙ ☙ ☙ ☙ ☙

23 By faith Moses, when he was born, was hidden for three months by his parents, because he *was* a beautiful child; and they were not afraid of the direction of the king.
24 By faith Moses, when he had become great, refused to be called the son of Pharaoh's daughter,

IV. Hold Fast to Christ — Hebrews 11:23–29

> 25 choosing rather to be co-mistreated with the people of God than to have the enjoyment of sin temporarily,
> 26 esteeming the reproach of Christ greater riches than the treasures of Egypt, for he was looking to the recompense.
> 27 By faith he left behind Egypt, not fearing the indignation of the king; for he endured as seeing the unseen *One*.
> 28 By faith he did the Passover and the sprinkling of the blood, that he who destroyed the firstborn might not touch them.
> 29 By faith they went through the Red Sea as though through dry land, and the Egyptians, when they made the attempt, were swallowed up.

Not just the patriarchs, but also the great **Moses** walked by faith. The element of faith in his life began almost as soon as **he was born**, for he **was hidden for three months by his parents**, in defiance of Pharaoh's order to have all the male infants slain (Ex. 1:15f), for they **were not afraid of** this **direction of the king**. His parents saw that **he *was* a beautiful child**, which they took as a sign of his favor with God and of his special destiny, and therefore for three months they concealed him. Crying infants are difficult to keep hidden forever, though, and so after this time, his parents in faith committed him to the hand of God, setting him adrift on the Nile River in a basket of reeds, trusting that God would preserve him. This God did, and he was found and raised by one of Pharaoh's daughters in the royal court.

But the hand of God was indeed upon this man of faith, and **when he** had grown up and **had become great**, Moses forswore his royal birthright. He **refused to be called the son of Pharaoh's daughter** any longer, but sided with his ancestral people, **choosing rather to be co-mistreated with the people of God than to have the enjoyment of sin temporarily**. Moses could have stayed in the royal court, enjoying a life of privilege and ease. This would have involved **sin**, for it would have meant turning his back on God and His people. But Moses would have none of it. He joined Israel in their suffering and struggle, even striking and killing an Egyptian who was abusing one of them (Ex. 2:11f). In doing so, he chose to share their **reproach** and their downtrodden fate. But this he freely did, even if it meant forfeiting all **the treasures of Egypt** which were his by birthright, **for he was looking to** God's eternal **recompense**.

This reproach upon Israel and Moses is described by our author as **the reproach of Christ**, since Jesus later experienced reproach as a result of doing the will of God. By describing Moses' choice to side with God even if it involved suffering as **the reproach of Christ**, our author identifies this reproach with the suffering his Jewish Christian readers were called to undergo. For the sake of Christ, they too must side with God, even if it meant forswearing the national loyalties into which they were born. Moses left his (Egyptian) family for the sake of God, and the readers of the epistle must be willing to leave their (Jewish) families for His sake also.

Having chosen to side with the God of the Hebrews, **by faith** Moses **left behind Egypt**, completely abandoning his former life. Exodus speaks of Pharaoh's wrath and his determination to have Moses killed (Ex. 2:15). But Moses was not daunted by this. **He endured** all the tribulations that befell him, **not fearing the indignation of the king**, but seeking his destiny in Midian, finding God at the burning bush and returning again to Egypt to defy Pharaoh to his face (Ex. 2:15f; 3:1f; 5:1). He did this because he could **see the unseen *One***, beholding with the eyes of faith the invisible God of Israel.

And Moses continued to put his faith in the unseen God in his striving with Pharaoh. **By faith he did the** first **Passover and the sprinkling of blood, that** the angel of death **who destroyed the firstborn might not touch** the children of Israel (Ex. 12). After this, Pharaoh the king relented, and they left Egypt—only to have Pharaoh change his mind and send his armies after them. And even in this hour of need, Moses' faith did not fail him. For **by faith** Israel **went through the Red Sea as though through dry land.**

IV. Hold Fast to Christ — Hebrews 11:30–31

This miracle depended entirely on their faith and loyalty to their God, and this was shown by the fact that **the Egyptians, when they made the attempt, were swallowed up** by the waters and drowned (Ex. 14).

Thus all of Moses' life involved faith in God's future reward. His parents surrendered him to the waters of the Nile, having faith that God would rescue and keep him. Moses himself renounced his Egyptian heritage, having faith that God would direct him. He kept the Passover with its sprinkling of the blood above the Israelite doorlintels, having faith that Israel would indeed be spared. He stretched out his staff over the Red Sea in their hour of crisis, having faith that the sea would part and that it would return again, drowning their foes. All of his life was a witness to the wisdom of enduring the present trial for the sake of future recompense.

---

30 By faith the walls of Jericho fell, after they had been encircled for seven days.
31 By faith Rahab the prostitute did not co-perish with those who disobeyed, after she had welcomed the spies with peace.

And this principle of faith was not just for Moses. It continued as the operative principle of salvation in all Israel's history. Even after the liberation from Egypt, it brought victories to Israel. When Israel entered the Promised Land and Joshua besieged Jericho, **the walls of Jericho fell** before them by the power of God **after they had been encircled for seven days** (Josh. 6). Israel marched about the city for seven days, blowing their trumpets, having **faith** that God would topple the walls and expose the city to their assault. And so it was. While they marched, day after day, there was no evidence that God would act. They simply had to trust His promise. And that faith brought victory.

After the city had fallen, faith continued to work salvation—and not just for Israel, but even for the pagan **Rahab the prostitute,** who had sided with the God of Israel and **welcomed the spies with**

peace when they came to reconnoiter (Josh. 2:1f; 6:22f). She put her faith in Israel's God, and thus **did not co-perish with those who disobeyed** or share their doom. Like her pagan countrymen who had **disobeyed** God through their idolatry, Rahab and her family should have been destroyed too. But she had chosen to side with the God of the Hebrews, and this faith proved to be her salvation. She remained with her family inside her house when Jericho fell, safe from the carnage ensuing outside. Faith brought salvation and life to her also.

ॐ ॐ ॐ ॐ ॐ

32 And what more shall I say? For time will fail me if I describe about Gideon, Barak, Samson, Jephthah, both David and Samuel and the prophets,

33 who by faith defeated kingdoms, worked righteousness, obtained promises, shut up the mouths of lions,

34 quenched the power of fire, fled the mouth of the sword, were made powerful from weakness, became strong in war, *caused* foreign camps to fall.

35 Women received their dead by resurrection, and others were tortured, not welcoming their release, that they might attain a better resurrection;

36 and others received experience of mockings and scourgings; still *others received experience* of chains and prisons.

37 They were stoned, they were sawn in two; they died, murdered by the sword; they went around in sheepskins, in goatskins, lacking, afflicted, mistreated;

38 (of whom the world was not worthy), wandering in deserts and mountains and caves and holes in the earth.

IV. Hold Fast to Christ   Hebrews 11:32–40

> 39 And all these, having been witnessed to through *their* faith, did not receive back the promise,
> 40 because God had foreseen something better for us, so that apart from us they should not be perfected.

Our author now declines to review every instance of saving faith in Israel's history, for **time** would **fail** him **if** he **described about** all those examples. Instead, he simply mentions names and events in order to give some indication of how sweeping was this principle of faith in salvation history.

Thus he mentions **Gideon** (Judg. 6–8), who liberated Israel from the Midianites, trusting in divine aid against an overwhelming enemy. He mentions **Barak** (Judg. 4–5), who wrought a similar victory against the superior force of the Canaanites. (It would seem that our author mentions Gideon before Barak because Gideon was the better known, even though he was chronologically later than Barak.) He mentions **Samson** (Judg. 13–16), who relied on supernatural strength from God in his many exploits against the Philistines. He mentions **Jephthah** (Judg. 11–12), who trusted in God's victory over the Ammonites as the response to his promise to sacrifice the first thing that emerged from his door. He mentions **both David and Samuel and the prophets**, meaning by this all the heroes of Israel in the historical books of the Old Testament (mentioning David first as the most illustrious of them). These also accomplished their feats of heroism only because they relied on the power of the God of Israel and found their faith in Him was rewarded.

After mentioning these few names, our author mentions a series of heroic feats, all the result of faith. Some, such as Moses, **defeated kingdoms**, such as that of Sihon and Og (Num. 21:21f). Some **worked righteousness**, as Daniel did when he vindicated the innocence of Susanna (Susanna 44f). Some **obtained promises**, as David did when God promised him that He would make of his house an everlasting dynasty (2 Sam. 7). Daniel **shut the mouths of lions** (Dan. 6); his companions Shadrach, Meshach, and Abednego **quenched the power of fire** by their faith (Dan. 3). Some, such as

Elijah and Elisha, escaped and **fled the mouth of the sword** when God delivered them from those who sought to slay them (1 Kin. 19:2f; 2 Kin. 6:31f).

Gideon and Samson **were made powerful from weakness**, as God gave them strength to triumph over their foes (Judg. 6, 16). David **became strong in war** (2 Sam. 8); others such as Judith *caused* foreign armies or **camps to fall** (Judith 13). **Women received their dead** back **by resurrection** as the prophets Elijah and Elisha restored them (1 Kin. 7; 2 Kin. 4). **Others,** such as Eleazar and the seven Maccabean martyrs, **were tortured, not welcoming** the **release** that could have been theirs if they apostatized, but keeping their faith **that they might attain a better resurrection** (4 Maccabees).

Others, such as Jeremiah, **received experience of mockings and scourgings** as the reward for their faithfulness to God (Jer. 20); **still** *others received experience* **of chains and prisons**. Men such as Zechariah the son of Jehoiada **were stoned** to death (2 Chr. 24:20–21). Isaiah, according to tradition, was **sawn in two**. Men such as the prophets contemporary with Elijah died, murdered by the sword (1 Kin. 19:10). The Maccabean resistance **went around in sheepskins** and **in goatskins, wandering in deserts and mountains and caves and holes in the earth** (2 Macc. 5:27; 10:6), persecuted and **mistreated** by their generation. They were men **of whom the world was not worthy**, and so they lived apart from the world, belonging to the age to come.

All these men of old, from righteous Abel down to recent times, **having been witnessed to through** *their* **faith, did not receive back the promise** God made them. God **witnessed** to them that they were deserving of His glory, and He had promised it to them as their reward, yet they did **not receive** it. And why? **Because God had foreseen something better** for the Christians, so **that apart from** the Christians these elders **should not be perfected** or reach their goal. The Christians were promised the glory of God—the same glory He had promised to these men of old. And so God willed to give them all their rewards at the same time, in the age to come.

Thus the readers of the epistle must hold fast to their faith. The salvation they had been promised was a glorious one indeed—so

IV. Hold Fast to Christ — Hebrews 12:1–2

glorious as to be worth the wait on the part of the martyrs and confessors of all Israel's sacred history.

> ꙮ ꙮ ꙮ ꙮ ꙮ
>
> **12** 1 Therefore, since we *ourselves* have such a cloud of witnesses surrounding us, let us also put off every weight and the sin which clings to us, and let us run with endurance the race lying before us,
> 2 looking to Jesus, the Leader and Perfecter of the Faith, who for the joy laid before Him endured the Cross, despising the shame, and has sat at the right *hand* of the throne of God.

Our author now draws together all those in Israel's history who had "been witnessed to through their faith" (11:39). God had witnessed to them, giving them His approval. They now stood like so many **witnesses** themselves (Gr. *martus*, compare the English "martyr"), testifying to the Christians of the need for endurance. These men of old had endured and now awaited their final reward. They formed a great host, encouraging the Christians, with whose perfection and reward their own was bound up, to endure as well and so to reach the goal.

The image here is of the athletic games. The Christians addressed in the epistle were like runners in a race; the **cloud** or mass of people who were **witnesses** of the need for endurance were like spectators in the stands, **surrounding** the runners. Now was the time to **run with endurance the race lying before** them. As runners must not stop before crossing the finish line, so neither must the Christians cease their striving to serve Christ. Before the race, Olympic runners would **put off every weight**, every encumbering piece of clothing, in order to run to victory, and in the same way the Christians must put off **the sin which clings** to them and encumbers their efforts. Let them cast away all immorality and spiritual coarseness (see v. 16); let them run after saving sanctification (v. 14). Runners in the earthly race kept their eyes fixed on the finish line; let the disciples of the Lord **look to Jesus** and keep their eyes on Him. He is their **Leader**, the One who blazed the path for them (compare use in 2:10); He is their **Perfecter**, the One who will finally glorify all His faithful in the age to come—Old Testament saints as well as New Testament Christians (11:40).

Jesus had set the example for their race. He **endured the Cross, despising** its **shame**, refusing to let the certainty of that disgraceful death deter Him from reaching His goal. As He prayed in the Garden of Gethsemane, the Cross loomed before Him with all its shame and darkness, but Jesus still set His face to do the will of the Father. God has **laid before** Him all His glory and the authority of **sitting at the right *hand* of** His **throne**, and for this **joy**, Jesus **endured the Cross**. Now His disciples must do the same. The same race to glory was **lying before** them too, and they also must **run with endurance**, as their Lord had. Jesus awaited them at the finish line to crown them (and the saints of Israel before them) with His eternal glory—let them fix their eyes on Him and run to the end!

§IV.3. Accept Suffering as God's Sons (12:3–29)

> ༺ ༺ ༺ ༺ ༺
>
> 3 For contemplate Him who has endured such contradiction by sinners against Himself, so that you may not be worn out in your souls and faint.
> 4 You have not yet resisted to the point of *shedding* blood in your struggling against sin,

The temptation was to be **worn out in** their **souls** through persecution from their fellow Jews, and so collapse and **faint** away, and not cross that finish line. Instead, let them **contemplate Him who endured such contradiction** and opposition **by sinners against Himself**. Jesus had faced this same struggle. He knew what it was like to be misunderstood, to be slandered—even to be scourged and killed. Let them consider how much Christ endured and remember

IV. Hold Fast to Christ — Hebrews 12:5–11

that they had not yet endured anything like that. They had **not yet resisted to the point of** *shedding* **blood in** their **struggling against sin** and apostasy. They had suffered, it was true (10:32–34), but they had not yet suffered martyrdom and death, as their Lord had.

> ꙳ ꙳ ꙳ ꙳ ꙳
>
> 5 and you have overlooked the exhortation which is addressed to you as sons, "My son, do not make light of the discipline of the Lord, nor faint when you are reproved by Him,
>
> 6 "for *those* whom the Lord loves He disciplines, and He scourges every son whom He welcomes."
>
> 7 *It is* for discipline that you endure; God deals with you as with sons; for what son *is there* whom his father does not discipline?
>
> 8 But if you are without discipline, of which all have become partakers, then you are illegitimate and not sons.
>
> 9 Furthermore, we had fathers of our flesh as disciplinarians, and we respected them; will we not much rather submit to the Father of spirits and live?
>
> 10 For they disciplined us for a few days as seemed *best* to them, but He *does so* for our advantage, that we may partake of His holiness.
>
> 11 All discipline for the moment does not seem to be joyful, but sorrowful, yet to those who have been trained by it, afterwards it renders the peaceful fruit of righteousness.

And moreover, it was apparent from their wavering that they had forgotten and **overlooked the exhortation** in the Scripture **which is addressed** to them **as** God's **sons**. For it is written in the Greek Septuagint version of Proverbs 3:11–12, "**My son, do not make light of the discipline of the Lord, nor faint when you are**

reproved by Him, for *those* whom the Lord loves He disciplines, and He scourges every son whom He welcomes." God in this text reveals how He deals with those He loves as His sons.

Just as a father in those days who cared about the character of his sons and heirs would **discipline** and **scourge** or beat them to punish them for their offenses (compare Prov. 13:24; 19:18), so God also allows His children to undergo persecution and suffering. However much methods of discipline may have changed from the days of Solomon until now, it remains true that earthly fathers are always less concerned that their children avoid suffering than they are that their children grow up with integrity. And so it is with God. He also is less concerned that His children avoid suffering at all costs than He is that His children become holy. To undergo persecution from unbelievers is a part of the suffering He allows them to experience.

The readers of the epistle therefore should **not make light** of such **discipline** nor question God's goodness when such suffering comes. They should **not faint** when they are thus **reproved by Him** and when the fire of persecution begins to purge away their dross. That He allows such suffering is evidence that He is concerned to purify their hearts through adversity. God is simply **dealing with** them **as with sons**, giving them the **discipline** any father would give to his son and heir. Indeed, if they were **without** such **discipline**, they might well question whether God was truly concerned about their character and their holiness at all. Even in our earthly experience, we see that children who grow up spoiled and without any discipline are to be pitied. The parents of such children we do not praise as kind; rather, we blame them as too indulgent. In the ancient world, such indulgence was given only to **illegitimate** offspring **and not sons**.

Why should the Christian readers of the epistle blame God for their suffering? They **had fathers of** their **flesh** (that is, earthly fathers) **as disciplinarians**, and they **respected them**. They did not think their fathers too harsh when they disciplined them. Should they **not much rather submit to the Father of spirits**, their heavenly Father, **and live?** For their earthly fathers **disciplined** them **for a few days** (that is, for a brief space of time, when they were children)—and not always with supreme wisdom, but **as seemed *best* to them**,

IV. Hold Fast to Christ — Hebrews 12:12–17

according to their limited wisdom. Sometimes the punishment may therefore have been too much. But their heavenly Father disciplines them with absolute wisdom, so that it is all **for** their **advantage**, so that they **may partake of His holiness** and know true life.

That such suffering is all for our **advantage** may not be immediately apparent to those suffering at the time. The natural tendency of everyone is to run from suffering and to question God's goodness when the suffering comes. It is the same with the just punishment given by earthly fathers. In that case too, **all discipline for the moment does not seem to be joyful** and an occasion for celebrating the ultimate good it will do us. No child likes to be punished. Rather, the discipline appears to be **sorrowful** and grievous. But **to those who have been trained by it, afterwards** when they are grown, **it renders the peaceful fruit of righteousness**, and the grown-up child thanks the father for such lessons. In the same way, after such persecution has been endured, we will thank our Father for the holiness such experiences have bestowed on us (see 1 Pet. 4:1, 14).

---

12 Therefore, restore the slackened hands and the disabled knees,
13 and make straight paths for your feet, that the lame *part* be not turned aside, but rather be cured.
14 Pursue peace with everyone, and the sanctification without which no one will see the Lord,
15 overseeing that no one lacks the grace of God, that no root of bitterness springing up *cause* trouble, and by it many be defiled,
16 that there be no fornicator or profane *person* like Esau, who sold his own *right as* firstborn for one meal.
17 For you know that even afterwards, when he wanted to inherit the blessing, he was rejected, for he did not find a place of repentance, although he sought it out with tears.

Therefore, they must run the race with endurance. They must cease wavering in their loyalty to Christ and shrinking from the future suffering such loyalty will incur. They are like runners whose hands are hanging down, drooping and useless, and whose knees are sagging. If they try to run the race in such a state, they will not finish. They must stand up straight and true; they must gather up their courage, **restore the slackened hands and the disabled knees**. They must **make straight paths for** their **feet, that their lame** *part* may **be cured**. If they avoid the straight path of the Christian course and try to run in the crooked side paths of compromise, **the lame part** of their bodies will become worse still and **be turned aside**, totally out of joint.

In their community life, such renewed dedication to Christ means they must **pursue** and run after **peace with everyone and the sanctification without which no one will see the Lord**. Their spiritual slackness meant a moral slackness as well. In their worldliness, there had been temptations to quarreling with their neighbors, as well as to fornication and to moral callousness. Such things were incompatible with discipleship to Jesus and with inheriting the Kingdom of God. If they did not attain and manifest true **sanctification** and holiness, they would not finally **see the Lord** in joy on the Last Day (compare 1 Cor. 6:9–10).

So there must be in their midst **no fornicator** (Gr. *pornos*; cognate with *porneia*, fornication), no **profane** *person*, one who was unclean, wicked, besmirched with worldliness (Gr. *bebelos*, compare its use in Ezek. 21:25 LXX). As a Christian community, they must take care to **oversee** such things (Gr. *episcopeo*, compare its use in 1 Pet. 5:2). They must make sure that all are holy and **that no one** among them **lacks the grace of God** through a sinful life. Such unrepentant sinners, if they continue to be impenitent, are to be expelled from their midst so **that no root of bitterness springing up** *cause* **trouble and by it many be defiled**.

The image of the **root of bitterness** is drawn from Deuteronomy 29:18 LXX. There it speaks of the necessity of not allowing an apostate to dwell in the midst of Israel, lest such a one prove to be "a root springing up with gall and bitterness," causing his deadly idolatry to spread to others. In the same way, the Church must not allow the impenitent sinner to dwell in the midst of the community lest such a one *cause* **trouble** by his worldliness, **and by it many** others **be defiled**, embracing those sinful ways too. Moral laxity cannot be tolerated in the Church.

The potential troublemaker is compared to **Esau, who sold his own** *right as* **firstborn for one meal** (Gen. 25:27f). In the Judaism of that day, Esau was an image of coarse sensuality, a man of appetites, and was famous as a fornicator. It may be surmised that his wives who made life bitter for his parents (Gen. 26:34–35) shared the immoral ways of pagans. In the Jewish *Book of Jubilees*, his wives are portrayed as filled with "fornication and lust," and the Palestinian *Targum* (or liturgical paraphrase) of the story of Esau said that on the day he sold his birthright he committed five sins, one of which was fornication. Esau abides therefore as an image of the world with its fornication and lack of restraint.

Our author warns his readers against following such an example, for such sins had eternal consequences. They **knew** very well from the scriptural record that **even afterwards, when** Esau **wanted to inherit the blessing** of his father Isaac, **he was rejected**. His deed had proven irrevocable, and he **did not find a place of repentance** or a way to change his mind, **although he sought it out with tears**. It would be the same with immoral apostates from the Church. If one persisted in one's immorality and sin until the end, one would pay the price on the Last Day. On that day too there would be no way to change one's mind, and all one's tears of grief would prove useless. One would be lost to the Gehenna of fire, where one's tears would flow forever, along with the furious gnashing of teeth (Matt. 8:12). Let the Christian readers of the epistle learn from the tragedy of godless Esau and run in the way of holiness!

༄ ༄ ༄ ༄ ༄

18 For you have not come *near* to *a mountain* that may be touched, and to a burning fire, and to darkness and gloom and storm,
19 and to the noise of a trumpet, and to a voice of

> sayings which those who heard requested that not a word be added to them.
> 20 For they could not bear the order, "If even a beast touches the mountain, it will be stoned."
> 21 And so fearful was the sight that Moses said, "I am frightened and trembling."
> 22 But you have come *near* to Mount Zion and to the city of the living God, to the heavenly Jerusalem, and to myriads of angels,
> 23 to a festival and to the Church of the firstborn who are enrolled in the heavens, and to God the Judge of all, and to the spirits of the perfected righteous,
> 24 and to Jesus, the Mediator of a new covenant, and to the sprinkled Blood, which speaks better than *the blood* of Abel.

Our author concludes his main exhortation to endurance by a last contrast of the old covenant with the new, as typified by the two mountains, Mount Sinai and the heavenly Mount Zion. Mount Sinai typified Judaism, their ancestral faith. The divine holiness under this covenant was a forbidding holiness, one that inspired fear and served to keep men at bay. Men under this covenant encountered ***a mountain* that may be touched**, a tangible piece of ground in the Arabian peninsula, a thoroughly earthly provenance. During God's revelation of the Mosaic covenant there, Israel came to **a burning fire, and to darkness and gloom and storm, and to the noise of a trumpet, and to a voice of sayings** which could be audibly heard (Ex. 19:16f). All was earthly, consisting of the phenomena of this world.

And the holiness there served to keep men distant. The divine **voice** with its **sayings** and commands was such that **those who heard** it **requested that not a word be added to them** and that God speak no more words from Sinai, so terrifying was that voice (Ex. 20:18–19). More than that, the divine presence was so forbidding and threatening, the **order** was given that **"if even a beast touches**

IV. Hold Fast to Christ — Hebrews 12:18–24

the mountain, it will be stoned" (Ex. 19:12), and the people **could not bear** such terrifying holiness. **The sight** and spectacle was **so fearful** that even the great **Moses** himself later admitted to being **frightened and trembling** (Deut. 9:19)—and the Greek here is not simply the normal word for being afraid (*phobos*), but the more intensive *ekphobos*, "terrified." The holiness of the Jewish old covenant served to keep men away from God, not to draw men to Him.

And the Christian readers of the epistle had **not come *near*** to such a reality through their faith in Jesus. Instead they had come near to a different reality, a different mountain—the heavenly **Mount Zion, the city of the living God, the heavenly Jerusalem**. The earthly Zion was a symbol of God's heavenly dwelling, and it was this transcendent presence the Christians approached through the high-priesthood of Jesus. All the tribes of Israel were to go up to Jerusalem (Ps. 122:4), and all the disciples of Jesus could go up spiritually to approach **the living God** in His heavenly **city**. Through Christ, the holiness of God was no longer such as to keep men back. Formerly, it was too dangerous for sinful man to approach and look on the holy God (Ex. 33:20), but now God's holy presence was accessible through Christ.

In the Church's worship, Christians could come near to the highest and holiest realities of heaven. They could join in the worship of **myriads of angels** at the heavenly **festival**. The word translated *festival* is the Greek *paneguris*, which is used in secular Greek to denote the great public celebrations held in honor of the gods—a time of feasting and banquets, of wine and garlands and song (compare our English "panegyric," a song of praise). The angels continually hold such high festival to God in heaven, and it is this heavenly banquet that the Church joins in her eucharistic liturgy.

This heavenly reality is described further as **the Church of the firstborn who are enrolled in the heavens**. All Christians belong to this Church, whether still present in the body on earth or absent from the body and with the Lord in heaven. The Church on earth is a reflection of this transcendent assembly above, in that the earthly Church even now spiritually sits with the Lord in the heavenlies (Eph. 2:6) and has its eucharistic sacrifice centered there.

This gathering is called **the Church of the firstborn** because all Christians share the privileged status the firstborn sons used to have. In ancient days, it was the firstborn son who was the head of the family and who received a double share of the inheritance. Such privileged status is now shared by all the Christian people, as we are called to be co-heirs with Christ, the eternal Firstborn of the Father (Col. 1:15, 18; Rom. 8:17). As sharers in such dignity, our names are **enrolled in the heavens**, inscribed in God's register. Kings in those days kept a register of persons they wished to honor, who were the king's friends (compare Esther 6:1). This practice became the basis for the idea of Yahweh having such a heavenly register, a list of His favorites (Ex. 32:32; Mal. 3:16). This idea continued in the New Testament, with God being portrayed as keeping His favorites and His children **enrolled** in His Book **in the heavens** (compare Luke 10:20; Rev. 20:12). This privilege is shared by all disciples of Jesus.

Further, the Christians in their worship approached **God the Judge of all**, the One who presides over this heavenly assembly as the Sovereign of all the earth. He rejoices over His children, **the spirits of the perfected righteous** of Old Testament times. While they walked the earth, these **righteous** men and women could not know a true inner cleansing through the Law. Now that Jesus has come and has made an eternal offering for sin and has abolished death, these Old Testament saints can be **perfected** and cleansed, and their **spirits** can abide with God in the heavens.

That is because **Jesus, the Mediator of a new covenant**, remains in the heavens as their eternal intercessor, sacrifice, and propitiation. He is there to plead before God His **sprinkled Blood**. Under the Law, the high-priest sprinkled the blood of animals before God to assure access into His presence. Jesus' sacrifice on the Cross provides that **sprinkled Blood** for us, whereby we have access to God. And His Blood **speaks better than *the blood* of Abel**. Abel's blood cried to God for justice and vengeance upon Cain for his sin (Gen. 4:10); the Blood of Christ cries for mercy for penitent sinners.

It is to these intangible and heavenly realities that the Hebrew Christians came through Christ. This was a much better covenant, a higher and more glorious mountain. How could they slip back from the heavenly to the earthly, from Zion to Sinai, from the Christian Faith to Judaism?

> ॐ ॐ ॐ ॐ ॐ
> 25 See that you do not reject Him who is speaking. For if those did not flee away when they rejected Him who warned on earth, much less will we *ourselves do so* who turn away from Him *who warns* from the heavens.
> 26 His voice shook the earth then, but now He has promised, saying, "Yet once more I *Myself* will shake not only the earth, but also the heaven."
> 27 And this *word*, "Yet once more," makes plain the removal of what is shaken, as of what has been made, that what is not shaken may remain.

Given these higher realities, they must **see that** they **do not reject** God **who is speaking** to them through the Gospel. **For if those** under the Old Covenant **did not flee away** or escape **when they rejected Him who warned on earth, much less** will they as Christians (the *we* is emphatic in the Greek) escape if they **turn away** from God who now *warns* **from the heavens**. Apostasy from the God who thundered from the earthly Sinai was terrible enough. Apostasy from that same God who now warns from the heavenly Zion will be worse yet.

This superiority of the new covenant over the old, of the heavenly Zion over the earthly Sinai, is proved by another Scripture. For God **promised** in Haggai 2:6, **"Yet once more I *Myself* will shake not only the earth, but also the heaven."** Our author points out that in this scripture, God contrasts this impending and final shaking with the first and previous shaking when **His voice shook the earth** as He gave the Mosaic Covenant on Mount Sinai. That first shaking was a merely earthly one. Those at Mount Sinai experienced the earthly phenomenon of an earthquake. But the final and eschatological shaking would be of another order. It would **shake not only the earth,**

but also the heaven. That is (as our author stresses), it will be **the removal of what is shaken as of what has been made**, the complete overturning of the created order. This final cataclysm will come so **that what is not shaken may remain**. That is, everything that is temporal will give place to the eternal; the shakable and corruptible things of this age will give place to the unshakable and incorruptible things of the age to come, the eternal Kingdom of God.

Thus, this prophecy from Haggai **makes plain** the transcendent nature of the new covenant and the Kingdom of God. The Sinai covenant was earthly and could only shake the earth. The Kingdom brought in by Jesus will be a transcendent one and will be brought in when both the heavens and the earth are shaken and removed. How terrible to reject a God who offers such a Kingdom!

> ॐ ॐ ॐ ॐ ॐ
>
> 28 Therefore, since we receive an unshakable Kingdom, let us *give* thanks, by which we may worship God in a well-pleasing *way*, with reverence and awe,
> 29 for indeed our God *is* a consuming fire.

Here is the final conclusion to our author's main exhortation: **since we receive an unshakable Kingdom**, superior to the shakable realities of this age found under the Law, **let us give thanks** to God. The proper response to the gift of so great a salvation is gratitude. Rather than fall away from Christ and drift back into Judaism, let the readers of the epistle recognize the magnitude of the divine gift given them in Jesus and be thankful. It is through such enduring devotion to Jesus and such gratitude for His gift of salvation that they **worship God in a well-pleasing way**. This was the worship which was truly **well-pleasing** to God, not the carnal worship of offering bulls and goats. Acceptable worship was offered by the Church through Christ, not in the Temple through mortal priests.

And this worship was offered **with reverence and awe**. If the readers of the epistle could but appreciate all that had been done for them in Christ, their attitude would be one of breathless and prostrate wonderment. For their **God**, the One who *is* **a consuming fire** (compare Deut. 4:24), jealous of His glory, terrible to apostates, wonderful in His saints, that same God welcomes them into His presence and calls them home. What else can they do but rejoice with trembling (Ps. 2:11) and give Him thanks?

V

CONCLUSION
(13:1–25)

§V.1. Final Admonitions (13:1–19)

Having concluded his principal appeal, our author adds a few other words of admonition to the local community to which his epistle is addressed.

> **13** 1 Let brotherly-love remain.
> 2 Do not forget hospitality, for by this some have entertained angels unawares.
> 3 Remember the prisoners, as *if* co-prisoned *with them*, and those who are mistreated, as you yourselves also are in the body.

First and foremost, they are urged to love one another. As a Christian community, they were characterized by **brotherly-love** (Gr. *philadelphia*). They must **let** that love **remain** undiminished among them, for it was only by such mutual love that they would be recognizable as Christ's disciples at all (John 13:35).

This love is not just a feeling, however, devoid of practical out-working. If love truly inflamed their hearts, it would spill over the boundaries of their own enclosed community to reach others as well. Thus it is that they are urged **not** to **forget** the duty of **hospitality** (Gr. *philoxenia*—literally, "love for strangers"). The welcoming of travelers into one's home was a sacred duty and a way of life for the early Christian communities. In the absence of safe inns (the inns available in those days were notorious for their danger and immorality), the Christians relied on one another as they traveled. This, of course, led to some abusing such a network of hospitality, and later on rules were laid down for distinguishing between the true Christian sojourner and the sponging con artist. (Thus the *Didache* lays down in chapter 12 the rule that the visitor "shall not stay with you more than two or three days . . . [otherwise] he is trafficking upon Christ.")

It is possible that the readers of our epistle had been taken in by such men and were overly wary, determined not to be conned again, and were therefore reluctant to offer hospitality to anyone. This they must not do. They must not let the possible abuse deter them from the godly use. Hospitality had a long history among God's people and had always brought God's blessing. Indeed, **by this** act of hospitality some had **entertained angels unawares**. Our author is thinking of such examples as that of Abraham, when he received "three men" by the oaks of Mamre, unaware initially who his guests were (Gen. 18), and of Manoah and his wife, the parents of Samson, who received an angel, thinking only that he was a wandering "man of God" (Judg. 13). These had offered sacred hospitality and had received God's blessing in return. So would the readers of the epistle, their descendants.

Their love must go even further afield as they went out to visit prisoners and minister to them in prison, bringing food and words of encouragement. They must **remember the prisoners, as *if*** they were also **co-imprisoned *with them*** and shared their confinement. That is, the prisoners' plight must never be far from their thoughts and prayers. When they returned from the prison to their daily life, they must not, as can so easily happen, let the prisoners slip away utterly, so that they were "out of sight" and therefore "out of mind."

And not just the prisoners, but also any who were **mistreated**, such as those who experienced floggings (compare our Lord's words in Mark 13:9 about His disciples being "flogged in the synagogues"). Since the readers themselves **also** were **in the body**, they could imagine how these mistreated ones felt.

V. Conclusion — Hebrews 13:4–6

> ❧ ❧ ❧ ❧ ❧
>
> 4 *Let* marriage *be* honored among all, and *its* bed *be* undefiled; for fornicators and adulterers God will judge.
> 5 *Let* your way *of life be* not money-loving, being satisfied with what you have; for He Himself has said, "I will never desert you; I will never leave you behind,"
> 6 so that we have courage to say, "The Lord *is* my helper, I will not be afraid. What will man do to me?"

Other exhortations follow. They must ***let* marriage *be* honored among all**. That is, all must respect marriage with its jealous claims of exclusivity and must let *its* **bed *be* undefiled**. (It is grammatically possible to read this sentence as in the indicative mood—i.e. "marriage is honored among all and its bed is undefiled," but the subjunctive mood suits it better. Our author is not making a statement about the marriage bed, and saying it *is* undefiled; he is clearly warning his readers *not to defile* the marriage bed with adultery, **for fornicators and adulterers God will judge**. Such sin may go undetected by the spouse of the offending partner, but it will not escape the notice and judgment of God. All such sexual immorality will be judged by Him, either in this life or in the age to come. Let there be no fornicators like Esau among them (12:16).

Further, they must let their **way *of life be* not money-loving** (Gr. *aphilarguros*), free from grasping greed. Rather, they must be **satisfied with what** they **have**. This was a real temptation, especially if persecution had to some degree impoverished them and if their property had been seized (10:34). Fear would drive them to think too much about money and not to trust in the Lord. But they had God's own word for it that He would take care of them. **He Himself** had **said** in the Scriptures, **"I will never desert you; I will never leave you behind"** (Deut. 31:6). In its original context, this promise was given to Israel as they faced the challenge of battle before taking possession of the Promised Land. That was exactly the spiritual position of the Christians. They must also fight the good fight of faith before entering God's final rest (4:11). Because of God's promise, they too could fight undaunted; they too could **have courage to say** with the Psalmist, **"The Lord *is* my helper, I will not be afraid. What will** mere **man do to me?"** (Ps. 118:6). Man may take away his property (Heb. 10:34), but God would still provide.

> ꙮ ꙮ ꙮ ꙮ ꙮ
>
> 7 Remember those who led you, who spoke the Word of God to you; and observing *carefully* the end of their conduct, imitate *their* faith.
> 8 Jesus Christ *is* the same yesterday and today and forever.

There were many challenges to their faithful way of life, and as an inspiration and example for them, they should **remember those who led** them, who first **spoke the Word of God** to them, the eternal Gospel. This refers to the first generation of teachers and clergy. They were older when first converted to Christ and had by this time died, probably of old age. The readers of the epistle therefore could review their whole life. They could **observe *carefully*** and scrutinize them, examine their lives minutely (not just *theoreo*, Greek for "observe," but the more intensive *anathereo*, "to observe carefully"). They could see that **their conduct** was loving, full of service, pure, unmercenary. And they could see **the end** of such conduct (Gr. *ekbasis*, "exit"; compare its use in Wisdom 2:17 for the death of the righteous and his exit from life). They could see how such a life led to a glorious death. They could **imitate** such **faith**, confident that, if they did, they too would receive such a reward. For the **Jesus Christ** proclaimed by these teachers is **the same yesterday and today and forever**. He never changes, and He rewards all who faithfully serve Him, whatever their generation.

V. Conclusion — Hebrews 13:9–14

> ৯ ৯ ৯ ৯ ৯
>
> 9 Do not be carried off by various and strange teachings; for *it is* good for the heart to be confirmed by grace, not by foods through which those walking *thus* were not profited.
> 10 We have an altar, from which those who worship *at* the Tent have no authority to eat.
> 11 For the bodies of the living *things* whose blood is brought into the *Holy* of Holies by the high-priest as *an offering* for sin are burned up outside the camp.
> 12 Therefore Jesus also, that He might sanctify the people through His own Blood, suffered outside the gate.
> 13 So then let us go out to Him outside the camp, bearing His reproach.
> 14 For here we do not have a city that remains, but we are seeking for the coming one.

After referring to the unchanging Gospel lived and proclaimed by their founders and teachers, our author then warns his readers **not** to **be carried off by various and strange teachings**. What was the nature of these teachings? It is difficult to say with certainty. From the context they obviously affirmed that the inner **heart** of the believer was **confirmed** and strengthened **by foods**. It was a common Jewish practice to eat cultic meals together (the main ones being the Sabbath meals and the Passover meal), and these meals were fraught with religious significance.

I would suggest that in the increasingly apocalyptic days preceding the destruction of the Temple, a number of Jewish teachers were spreading the teaching that participation in these cultic meals was essential to salvation. The days leading up to the catastrophe in AD 70 were days of increasingly shrill and intense nationalism, in which one's Jewish identity was crucial. It was believed by many

Jews that all Israel would have a share in the age to come, and if the Messiah were expected to come soon and deliver Israel from the Roman threat, one's Jewish identity would be crucial to one's salvation.

I suggest (quite tentatively) that participation in these religious meals was invested with this saving significance. These **teachings** were **various**, for they were perhaps present in various forms (one rabbi teaching this variant of it, perhaps saying that the Passover was all that was required, another rabbi teaching a different variant, saying that participation in all such meals was essential). The teachings were condemned by our author as **strange** in that they were not only new, but also foreign to the deposit of faith laid down by the founding Christian teachers.

Over against such alien teachings, our author affirms that *it is* **good for the heart to be confirmed** and strengthened **by grace,** and not by anything physical and carnal such as Jewish **foods**. Participation in such cultic meals could add nothing to their salvation. Even in the past, **those walking** *thus* (i.e. paying strict attention to food laws) **were not profited** by it. The Mosaic food laws achieved their purpose in keeping Israel socially separate from the nations surrounding them, but they could **not profit** them by strengthening their hearts (nor were they ever intended to). Only God's **grace**, given in Christ, could do this.

To be sure, if the Christians of those increasingly nationalistic days held aloof from such meals, they might be rejected as traitors to the national Jewish cause and even refused access to the Temple sacrifices. But no matter. For the Christians **have an altar** to which no Jewish authority could bar them access—that Heavenly Altar from which they receive at their weekly Eucharists. And **those who worship** *at* **the** earthly **Tent have no authority to eat** from this Altar. Let the unbelieving Jews bar them from their altar in Jerusalem! These Jews are themselves barred by their unbelief from the true altar in heaven.

The Christian Jews, the readers of the epistle, should therefore not fear segregation from unbelieving Jewish countrymen nor tremble when ostracized by them. Such separation is inevitable.

V. Conclusion — Hebrews 13:15–16

For the bodies of the living *things*, the animals **whose blood is brought into the *Holy* of Holies by the high-priest as *an offering* for sin** on the Day of Atonement, **are burned up outside the camp** (Lev. 16:27). Christ fulfilled this sacrifice, as He fulfilled all the sacrifices of the Law, and it was the offering of His **Blood** that **sanctified the people**.

The details of this Day of Atonement ritual were typologically prophetic of Christ and His sacrifice on the Cross. As the bodies of the sacrifices were ejected from the midst of Israel to a place outside the camp on the Day of Atonement, **Jesus also suffered** on the Cross **outside the gate** of Jerusalem, rejected by the people of Israel. That is, Christ's rejection by Israel and His crucifixion outside the city was the unwitting fulfillment by Israel of their prophetic Law. As Christ suffered such reproach and disgrace, we also must **go out to Him outside the camp, bearing His reproach**. Christ was rejected by His people and disowned by them. The Christian readers of the epistle must be willing to share His shame and carry the same **reproach** He carried. They must joyfully accept it when their fellow Jews reject and disown them, for their Lord experienced the same rejection.

What did it matter if they were denied the fullness of the city of Jerusalem? Here on earth, in this age, they did **not have a city that remains**, that endures to the ages, that lasts to eternity. Jerusalem was an earthly city like all earthly cities, and like all cities, she would fall. As Christians they were **seeking for the coming** city, the eternal City of the living God, the heavenly Jerusalem that endures forever (12:22). That City would one day descend from heaven, adorned like a bride for her husband (Rev. 21:2). That was their city, and no one on earth could deny them access to its fullness.

> ૐ ૐ ૐ ૐ ૐ
> 15 Through Him, therefore, let us continually offer a sacrifice of praise to God, that is, *the* fruit of lips confessing His Name.
> 16 And do not forget doing good and sharing; for with such sacrifices God is well-pleased.

They must therefore be ready to stand with Jesus wherever He was, even in the place of disgrace. As Christians, they must stand together, at the Eucharist, not neglecting the weekly assembly (10:25), for they belonged to Jesus and to each other. **Through Him**, they must **continually**, week by week, **offer a sacrifice of praise** to God in their Eucharist. This was the true sacrifice that honored God and praised Him—not the blood of calves, but the **fruit of lips confessing His Name**. For in the Eucharist, the Name of God is confessed and lifted up. As the Psalmist said prophetically long ago, "I will praise the Name of God with song, and magnify Him with praise, and it will please God more than a young calf with horns and hoofs" (Ps. 69:30–31). It is the words of praise we offer in the Eucharist, making saving memorial of the Cross, which are the true sacrifice. It is this sacrifice which pleases God—not the offering of animals.

And this eucharistic praise is not unconnected with **such sacrifices** as **doing good and sharing**. The giving of alms, the visiting of the sick, and the sharing of food with the poor were an integral part of their life of worship, the practical result of it during the week. One's devotional worship finds daily expression in good deeds and kindness to the needy, and with such intangible sacrifices **God is well-pleased**. The Jewish Christians did not need access to the Temple to offer acceptable sacrifices to God.

> ꙮ ꙮ ꙮ ꙮ ꙮ
> 17 Obey those leading you and yield to them; for they keep awake for your souls, as those who will render an account. Let them do this with joy and not with groaning, for this *would be* unprofitable for you.

As a remedy against the temptation to apostatize, our author urges his readers to **obey those leading** them **and yield to them**. This submission to their presbyters and teachers would bind them all into one as all in the Christian community followed the godly lead of their clergy. In times of persecution and stress, the temptation is not only to scatter, it is also to quarrel (compare 12:14, with its exhortation to "pursue peace with everyone"), and it seems as if some of the readers were quarreling with their leaders. This they must not do.

For their leaders were like God's watchmen (compare Ezek. 3:17), set by Him over all in the community to **keep awake for** their **souls** (Gr. *agrupneo*; compare its use in Luke 21:36, and the cognate *agrupnia* in 2 Cor. 6:5, translated "sleeplessness"). They were to sleeplessly watch over every one of them, exhorting, encouraging, rebuking where necessary, praying that all might reach salvation. This was their mandate given to them by God, and to Him they would one day have to **render an account**. Should any be lost through their negligence, God would require it at their hand.

Men with such a responsibility should be allowed to do their work **with joy and not with groaning**. If the readers of the epistle fought and quarreled with their leaders, causing them to fulfill their work through such discouragement and grief, that would be **unprofitable** to the readers. They could only benefit from such pastoral care if all the community was united around their clergy.

༃ ༃ ༃ ༃ ༃

18 Pray for us, for we are persuaded that we have a good conscience, wanting to conduct ourselves well in all things.
19 And I urge you all the more to do this that I may be restored to you the sooner.

Our author comes now to his final words and prefaces them with a request for prayer. In asking his readers to **pray for** him (the literary plural is used), he is **persuaded that** he **has a good conscience** and **wants to conduct** himself **well in all things**. That is, he is a man of integrity, and so his readers' prayers for him to be blessed will not be in vain (as they would be if he were a hypocrite). And what he wants most from their prayers is that he **may be restored** to them **the sooner**. As suggested in the Introduction, the author was probably writing from Rome and was anxious, through their prayers and the mercy of God, to return safely to them in Palestine.

§V.2. Concluding Blessing (13:20–21)

> ৵ ৵ ৵ ৵ ৵
> 20 Now may the God of peace, who brought up from the dead Jesus our Lord, the great Shepherd of the sheep, through the Blood of the eternal covenant,
> 21 prepare you with every good thing to do His will, working in us what is well-pleasing before Him, through Jesus Christ, to whom be the glory to ages of ages. Amen.

Our author does not end without invoking the blessing of God on them. It is possibly because of their quarreling that God is invoked as **the God of peace**. And this God, the God of Israel, the God of their fathers, is none other than He **who brought up from the dead Jesus our Lord, the great Shepherd of the sheep, through the Blood of the eternal** new **covenant**, God's true covenant with Israel. Jesus is described as their true **Shepherd**, the One who would pastor, protect, and feed them. And His victory, when He was **brought up from the dead**, was only **through** His own **Blood**, after He had been rejected by Israel. The implication is that Christ reached His victorious goal only through suffering—and His disciples would too.

What our author prays for is for God to prepare them with every good thing. The word rendered *prepare* is the Greek *katarizo*. It is used in 11:3 for God's preparing and creation of the heavens, and in Mark 1:19 for the mending of nets as a preparation for their being used again. The thought here is one of restoration. The Christians were embattled, weary, and beginning to scatter and quarrel. But God would provide all they lacked, all they needed, giving them **every good thing** and every spiritual gift so they could do His will. It was through *His* power that they would be mended and healed. *He* would **work in** them **what was well-pleasing before Him,** helping them to persevere in their faith and serve Him in holiness, and He would do this **through Jesus Christ** as they clung to Him in loyalty. To this God **be the glory to ages of ages**.

(It is grammatically possible that the antecedent of this last clause is Jesus Christ, so that our author ascribes glory to Jesus. However, I think it more likely that the antecedent is God, the subject of the whole blessing, for a doxological ascription to God is characteristic of such Jewish blessings. Thus the praise is to God the Father, through Jesus Christ; compare v. 15.)

§V.3. Final Greetings (13:22–25)

> 22 But I exhort you, brothers, bear with this word of exhortation, for I have written to you briefly.
> 23 Know that our brother Timothy has been released, with whom, if he comes soon, I will see you.
> 24 Greet all those leading you and all the saints. Those from Italy greet you.
> 25 Grace *be* with you all.

Our author reaches his final words. He **exhorts** his **brothers** in Christ to **bear with this word of exhortation**—that is, to try to grasp its full meaning. After all, he had only **written** to them **briefly**, and it should not be difficult to fathom and understand all he has said.

Final news is passed on. He wants them to **know that** their **brother Timothy** (the companion of St. Paul) had been recently **released** from prison. **If he comes soon** to them in Palestine, our author **will see** them, for he intends to come soon, whether with Timothy or not. We have here a fine example of the Christian communication grapevine with news being passed across the miles. This reveals how important relationships are in the Church. Timothy's fate is not a matter of indifference to others in faraway Palestine; all are one in Christ.

The readers are bidden to **greet all those leading** them and indeed **all the saints**, the rank and file of the Christian community there. (We note again the concern for unity.) **Those** believers **from Italy** who were in Rome with him **greet** them too. Our author ends his brief exhortation with a commendation, bidding God's **grace** upon them **all**.

About the Author

Archpriest Lawrence Farley currently pastors St. Herman of Alaska Orthodox Church (OCA) in Langley, B.C., Canada. He received his B.A. from Trinity College, Toronto, and his M.Div. from Wycliffe College, Toronto. A former Anglican priest, he converted to Orthodoxy in 1985 and studied for two years at St. Tikhon's Orthodox Seminary in Pennsylvania. In addition to the books in the Orthodox Bible Study Companion series, he has also published *The Christian Old Testament: Looking at the Hebrew Scriptures through Christian Eyes; A Song in the Furnace: The Message of the Book of Daniel; Unquenchable Fire: The Traditional Christian Teaching about Hell; A Daily Calendar of Saints: A Synaxarion for Today's North American Church; Let Us Attend: A Journey Through the Orthodox Divine Liturgy; One Flesh: Salvation through Marriage in the Orthodox Church; The Empty Throne: Reflections on the History and Future of the Orthodox Episcopacy;* and *Following Egeria: A Visit to the Holy Land through Time and Space.*

Visit www.ancientfaithradio.com to listen to Fr. Lawrence Farley's regular podcast, "No Other Foundation: Reflections on Orthodox Theology and Biblical Studies."

A Complete List of the Books in the Orthodox Bible Study Companion Series

The Gospel of Matthew
Torah for the Church
- Paperback, 400 pages, ISBN 978-0-9822770-7-2

The Gospel of Mark
The Suffering Servant
- Paperback, 280 pages, ISBN 978-1-888212-54-9

The Gospel of Luke
Good News for the Poor
- Paperback, 432 pages, ISBN 978-1-936270-12-5

The Gospel of John
Beholding the Glory
- Paperback, 376 pages, ISBN 978-1-888212-55-6

The Acts of the Apostles
Spreading the Word
- Paperback, 352 pages, ISBN 978-1-936270-62-0

The Epistle to the Romans
A Gospel for All
- Paperback, 208 pages, ISBN 978-1-888212-51-8

First and Second Corinthians
Straight from the Heart
- Paperback, 319 pages, ISBN 978-1-888212-53-2

Words of Fire
The Early Epistles of St. Paul to the Thessalonians and the Galatians
- Paperback, 172 pages, ISBN 978-1-936270-02-6

The Prison Epistles
Philippians – Ephesians – Colossians – Philemon
- Paperback, 224 pages, ISBN 978-1-888212-52-5

Shepherding the Flock
The Pastoral Epistles of St. Paul the Apostle to Timothy and Titus
- Paperback, 144 pages, ISBN 978-1-888212-56-3

The Epistle to the Hebrews
High Priest in Heaven
• Paperback, 184 pages, ISBN 978-1-936270-74-3

Universal Truth
The Catholic Epistles of James, Peter, Jude, and John
• Paperback, 232 pages, ISBN 978-1-888212-60-0

The Apocalypse of St. John
A Revelation of Love and Power
• Paperback, 240 pages, ISBN 978-1-936270-40-8

Other Books by the Author

The Christian Old Testament
Looking at the Hebrew Scriptures through Christian Eyes
Many Christians see the Old Testament as "the other Testament": a source of exciting stories to tell the kids, but not very relevant to the Christian life. *The Christian Old Testament* reveals the Hebrew Scriptures as the essential context of Christianity, as well as a many-layered revelation of Christ Himself. Follow along as Fr. Lawrence Farley explores the Christian significance of every book of the Old Testament.
• Paperback, 200 pages, ISBN 978-1-936270-53-8

A Song in the Furnace
The Message of the Book of Daniel
The Book of Daniel should be read with the eyes of a child. It's a book of wonders and extremes—mad kings, baffling dreams with gifted interpreters, breathtaking deliverances, astounding prophecies—with even what may be the world's first detective stories added in for good measure. To argue over the book's historicity, as scholars have done for centuries, is to miss the point. In *A Song in the Furnace*, Fr. Lawrence Farley reveals all the wonders of this unique book to the receptive eye.
• Paperback, 248 pages, ISBN 978-1-944967-31-4

A Daily Calendar of Saints
A Synaxarion for Today's North American Church
Popular biblical commentator and church historian Fr. Lawrence Farley turns his hand to hagiography in this collection of lives of saints, one or more for each day of the calendar year. His accessible prose and contemporary approach make these ancient lives easy for modern Christians to relate to and understand.
• Paperback, 304 pages, ISBN 978-1-944967-41-3

Unquenchable Fire
The Traditional Christian Teaching about Hell
The doctrine of hell as a place of eternal punishment has never been easy for Christians to accept. The temptation to retreat from and reject the Church's traditional teaching about hell is particularly strong in our current culture, which has demonstrably lost its sense of sin. Fr. Lawrence Farley examines the Orthodox Church's teaching on this difficult subject through the lens of Scripture and patristic writings, making the case that the existence of hell does not negate that of a loving and forgiving God.
• Paperback, 240 pages, ISBN 978-1-944967-18-5

Let Us Attend
A Journey Through the Orthodox Divine Liturgy
Fr. Lawrence Farley provides a guide to understanding the Divine Liturgy, and a vibrant reminder of the centrality of the Eucharist in living the Christian life, guiding believers in a devotional and historical walk through the Orthodox Liturgy. Examining the Liturgy section by section, he provides both historical explanations of how the Liturgy evolved and devotional insights aimed at helping us pray the Liturgy in the way the Fathers intended.
• Paperback, 104 pages, ISBN 978-1-888212-87-7

One Flesh
Salvation through Marriage in the Orthodox Church
Is the Church too negative about sex? Beginning with this provocative question, Fr. Lawrence Farley explores the history of the Church's attitude toward sex and marriage, from the Old Testament through the Church Fathers. He persuasively makes the case both for traditional morality and for a positive acceptance of marriage as a viable path to theosis.
• Paperback, 160 pages, ISBN 978-1-936270-66-8

The Empty Throne
Reflections on the History and Future of the Orthodox Episcopacy
In contemporary North America, the bishop's throne in the local parish stands empty for most of the year. The bishop is an honored occasional guest rather than a true pastor of the local flock. But it was not always so, nor need it be so forever. Fr. Lawrence Farley explores how the Orthodox episcopacy developed over the centuries and suggests what can be done in modern times to bring the bishop back into closer contact with his flock.
• Paperback, 152 pages, ISBN 978-1-936270-61-3

Following Egeria
A Visit to the Holy Land through Time and Space
In the fourth century, a nun named Egeria traveled through the Holy Land and wrote an account of her experiences. In the twenty-first century, Fr. Lawrence

Farley followed partially in her footsteps and wrote his own account of how he experienced the holy sites as they are today. Whether you're planning your own pilgrimage or want to read about places you may never go, his account will inform and inspire you.
• Paperback, 160 pages, ISBN 978-1-936270-21-7

Three Akathists:
Akathist to Jesus, Light to Those in Darkness
• Staple-bound, 32 pages, ISBN 978-1-944967-33-8

Akathist to the Most Holy Theotokos, Daughter of Zion
• Staple-bound, 32 pages, ISBN 978-1-944967-34-4

Akathist to Matushka Olga Michael
• Staple-bound, 32 pages, ISBN 978-1-944967-38-3

For complete ordering information, visit our website: store.ancientfaith.com.

Other Books of Interest

The Orthodox Study Bible: Old and New Testaments
Featuring a Septuagint text of the Old Testament developed by outstanding Orthodox scholars, this Bible also includes the complete Orthodox canon of the Old Testament, including the Deuterocanon; insightful commentary drawn from the Christian writers of the first ten centuries; helpful notes relating Scripture to seasons of Christian feasting and fasting; a lectionary to guide your Bible reading through the Church year; supplemental Bible study articles on a variety of subjects; a subject index to the study notes to help facilitate Bible study; and more.
• Available in various editions. Visite store.ancientfaith.com for more details.

The Whole Counsel of God
An Introduction to Your Bible
by Stephen De Young
In *The Whole Counsel of God*, popular writer and podcaster Fr. Stephen De Young gives an overview of what the Bible is and what is its place in the life of an Orthodox Christian, correcting many Protestant misconceptions along the way. Issues covered include inspiration, inerrancy, the formation of the biblical canon, the various texts and their provenance, the place of Scripture within Orthodox Tradition, and how an Orthodox Christian should read, study, and interpret the Bible.
• Paperback, 128 pages, ISBN: 978-1-955890-19-9

The Names of Jesus
Discovering the Person of Jesus Christ through Scripture
by Fr. Thomas Hoko
In this book based on his popular podcast series of the same name, the late Fr. Thomas Hopko shares meditations on over 50 different names and titles used for Jesus in the Bible. Learn what each name uniquely has to tell us about the character of the Son of God, His role in our salvation, and the relationship we can choose to cultivate with Him.
• Paperback, 400 pages, ISBN 978-1-936-70-41-5

The Rest of the Bible
A Guide to the Old Testament of the Early Church
by Theron Mathis
A beautiful widow risks her life to defend her people while men cower in fear. A young man takes a journey with an archangel and faces down a demon in order to marry a woman seven times widowed. A reprobate king repents and miraculously turns back toward God. A Jewish exile plays a game of riddles in a Persian king's court. Wisdom is detailed and exalted. Christ is revealed.

These and many other stories make up the collection of writings explored

in this book—authentic books of the Bible you've probably never read. Dubbed "Apocrypha" and cut from the Bible by the Reformers, these books of the Greek Old Testament were a vital part of the Church's life in the early centuries, and are still read and treasured by Orthodox Christians today. *The Rest of the Bible* provides a brief and intriguing introduction to each of these valuable texts, which St. Athanasius termed "the Readables."
• Paperback, 128 pages, ISBN 978-1-936270-15-6

Christ in the Psalms
by Patrick Henry Reardon
A highly inspirational book of meditations on the Psalms by one of the most insightful and challenging Orthodox writers of our day. Avoiding both syrupy sentimentality and arid scholasticism, *Christ in the Psalms* takes the reader on a thought-provoking and enlightening pilgrimage through this beloved "Prayer Book" of the Church. Which psalms were quoted most frequently in the New Testament, and how were they interpreted? How has the Church historically understood and utilized the various psalms in her liturgical life? How can we perceive the image of Christ shining through the psalms? Lively and highly devotional, thought-provoking yet warm and practical, *Christ in the Psalms* sheds a world of insight upon each psalm, and offers practical advice for how to make the Psalter a part of our daily lives.
• Paperback, 328 pages, ISBN 978-1-888212-21-7

Christ in His Saints
by Patrick Henry Reardon
In this sequel to *Christ in the Psalms,* Patrick Henry Reardon once again applies his keen intellect to a topic he loves most dearly. Here he examines the lives of almost one hundred and fifty saints and heroes from the Scriptures—everyone from Abigail to Zephaniah, Adam to St. John the Theologian. This well-researched work is a veritable cornucopia of Bible personalities: Old Testament saints, New Testament saints, "Repentant saints," "Zealous saints," "Saints under pressure" . . . they're all here, and their stories are both fascinating and uplifting. But *Christ in His Saints* is far more than just a biblical who's who. These men and women represent that ancient family into which, by baptism, all believers have been incorporated. Together they compose that great "cloud of witnesses" cheering us on and inspiring us through word and deed.
• Paperback, 320 pages, ISBN 978-1-888212-68-6

For complete ordering information, visit our website: store.ancientfaith.com.

We hope you have enjoyed and benefited from this book. Your financial support makes it possible to continue our nonprofit ministry both in print and online. Because the proceeds from our book sales only partially cover the costs of operating **Ancient Faith Publishing** and **Ancient Faith Radio**, we greatly appreciate the generosity of our readers and listeners. Donations are tax deductible and can be made at **www.ancientfaith.com**.

To view our other publications,
please visit our website: **store.ancientfaith.com**

Bringing you Orthodox Christian music, readings,
prayers, teaching, and podcasts 24 hours a day since 2004 at
www.ancientfaith.com

www.ingramcontent.com/pod-product-compliance
Lightning Source LLC
Chambersburg PA
CBHW030328100526
44592CB00010B/605